Sourdough Discard Recipes Cookbook 2025

The Complete Zero-Waste Guide for Busy Moms and Families to Craft Delicious, Nutritious Delights With All-Natural Ingredients

Nancy Strain

Copyright © 2024 by Nancy Strain. All rights reserved.

No part of this book may be reproduced, distributed, or transmitted in any form or by any means, including photocopying, recording, or other electronic or mechanical methods, without the prior written permission of the publisher, except in the case of brief quotations embodied in critical reviews and certain other non-commercial uses permitted by copyright law.

NOTE: Scan the QR code on the last page of this book to get access to your Bonuses

TABLE OF CONTENTS

INTRODUCTION 9
    The Art of Zero-Waste Baking with Sourdough 9
    Benefits of Sourdough Discard – Flavor, Nutrition, and Sustainability 9
    Essentials for Sourdough Success – Tools, Tips, and Tricks 10
    Maintaining and Storing Your Sourdough Discard 11

Chapter 1: Morning Delights to Start Your Day Right 13
    Apple Cinnamon Morning Muffins 14
    Classic Sourdough Bagels 14
    Banana Nut Bread with a Twist 15
    Wholesome Breakfast Burritos 16
    Lemon Poppy Seed Muffins 17
    Cornbread Pancakes 18
    Sourdough Spinach Quiche 18
    Fluffy Discard Pancakes 19
    Warm Cinnamon Rolls 20
    Zucchini Morning Loaf 21
    Dutch Baby with Berries 21
    Morning Glory Muffins 22
    Breakfast Casserole 23
    Sourdough Pop-Tarts 23
    Blueberry Oat Bars 24
    Savory Waffles 25
    Nutty Cereal Bars 26
    French Toast Loaf 26
    Pumpkin Spice Scones 27
    Frittata with Sourdough Base 28
    Chocolate Chip Muffins 28
    Cheese and Herb Breakfast Biscuits 29
    Breakfast Cookies with Nuts 30
    Sourdough Crepes 30

Sourdough Crepes ... 31

Chapter 2: Artisan Breads & Savory Rolls ... 33

- Everyday Sourdough Loaf ... 34
- Seeded Multigrain Bread ... 34
- Olive Herb Focaccia ... 35
- Classic French Baguettes ... 36
- Jalapeño Cheddar Bread ... 36
- Sweet Potato Dinner Rolls ... 37
- Soft and Chewy Brioche ... 38
- Savory Spinach Dip Bread Bowl ... 38
- Pumpernickel Bread ... 39
- Rustic Potato Loaf ... 40
- Honey Whole Wheat Bread ... 40
- Garlic Knots ... 41
- Sourdough Pretzel Bites ... 41
- Cheddar Biscuits ... 42
- Buttery Brioche Rolls ... 43
- Herb Cracker Breads ... 43
- Apple Cinnamon Quick Bread ... 44
- Rye Bread ... 44
- Cranberry Almond Loaf ... 45
- Chocolate Babka ... 46
- Rustic Country Bread ... 46
- Potato Focaccia ... 47
- Cinnamon Raisin Swirl Bread ... 48
- Quinoa Bread ... 48
- Garlic Parmesan Breadsticks ... 49
- Soft Hamburger Buns ... 50
- Pumpkin Quick Bread ... 50
- Spinach and Herb Rolls ... 51
- Oatmeal Bread ... 52
- Olive and Sun-Dried Tomato Bread ... 52

Chapter 3: Irresistible Bites & Savory Treats ... 55

- Crispy Parmesan Cheese Straws 56
- Herbed Garlic Breadsticks 56
- Soft Pretzel Bites 57
- Mozzarella Stuffed Rolls 58
- Kale and Herb Chips 59
- Sourdough Dumplings 59
- Savory Popovers with Cheddar 60
- Crab Cakes with Sourdough 60
- Mediterranean Flatbreads 61
- Spinach and Feta Turnovers 62
- Sourdough Empanadas 62
- Flatbread with Olive Tapenade 63
- Cheesy Breadsticks 64
- Stuffed Bread Rolls 64
- Grissini Sticks 65
- Sourdough Pizza Bites 65
- Roasted Red Pepper Crackers 66
- Stuffed Mini Peppers with Sourdough 67
- Herbed Cheese Straws 67
- Samosas with Sourdough Pastry 68

Chapter 4: Comforting Main Dishes 71

- Hearty Burrito Bowls 72
- BBQ Chicken Flatbread 73
- Savory Chicken Pot Pie 75
- Sourdough Pierogi 76
- Stromboli with Italian Herbs 78
- Discard Gnocchi 79
- Stromboli with Italian Herbs 81
- Creamy Alfredo Pasta with Sourdough 82
- Recipe 8: Vegetarian Lasagna with Sourdough Crust 83
- Veggie Burgers with Sourdough Buns 86
- Calzones with Mixed Cheese 87
- Cheesy Enchiladas 88

Fish Tacos with Sourdough Tortillas 89

Meatball Subs on Sourdough Hoagies 90

Tomato Basil Sourdough Pasta 91

Chapter 5: Delectable Desserts 93

Classic Brownies with a Sourdough Twist 94

Apple Cinnamon Fritters 94

Banana Cream Pie 95

Rich Chocolate Babka 96

Gingerbread Cookies 97

Lemon Drizzle Cake 98

Sourdough Carrot Cake 99

Coconut Macaroons 100

Sticky Toffee Pudding 101

Chocolate Chip Cookies 101

Double Chocolate Cake 102

Blueberry Buckle 103

Raspberry Bars 104

Biscotti with Almonds 104

Donuts with Sourdough Base 105

Boston Cream Pie 106

Apple Pie with Sourdough Crust 107

Pumpkin Pie with Sourdough Crust 107

Tiramisu with Sourdough Ladyfingers 108

Chocolate Truffles 109

Lemon Bars 109

Peach Cobbler 110

Mug Cake 111

Cherry Clafoutis 111

Sweet Biscuit Shortcake 112

Chapter 6: Versatile Doughs & Batters 115

All-Purpose Discard Dough 116

Basic Bread Dough 116

Empanada Dough 117

Soft Pizza Dough 117

Pastry Dough for Pies 118

Crepe Batter 118

Pancake Batter with Sourdough 119

Chapter 7: Decadent Delights & Gourmet Bites 121

Cranberry Orange Scones 122

Chocolate Truffle Bites 123

Mini Sourdough Cheesecakes 123

Pumpkin Spice Scones 124

Savory Samosas 124

Blueberry Clafoutis 125

Tiramisu with Sourdough Layers 125

Chapter 8: Guilt-Free Gluten-Free Goodies 127

Gluten-Free Sourdough Pretzels 128

Gluten-Free Bagels 129

Gluten-Free Biscuits 130

Gluten-Free Cornbread 132

Gluten-Free Wraps 133

Gluten-Free Focaccia 134

Gluten-Free Pancakes 135

Gluten-Free Breakfast Muffins 136

Conclusion 139

INTRODUCTION

The Art of Zero-Waste Baking with Sourdough

The practice of zero-waste baking has transformed kitchens, bringing new meaning to sustainable cooking. As more families embrace this approach, sourdough discard becomes a powerful tool to minimize waste, enhance creativity, and maximize nutritional value in everyday meals. Sourdough discard is the portion of starter typically removed during feeding to keep the balance of yeast and bacteria active and manageable. Instead of tossing this portion, home bakers can repurpose it, transforming a would-be waste product into a variety of delicious and healthful recipes. This book opens the door to a world of culinary potential where sourdough discard becomes a staple ingredient for creative, nutritious, and sustainable cooking.

By utilizing sourdough discard, bakers not only reduce waste but also bring a distinct flavor profile and nutritional boost to recipes that might otherwise rely on commercial yeast or conventional leaveners. Every family, especially busy moms and active households, can benefit from the flexibility and nutritional quality that sourdough discard offers. It has an adaptable nature that works across sweet, savory, and everything in between, allowing it to pair well with a range of other ingredients. For many, embracing zero-waste baking with sourdough discard becomes a commitment to sustainability—a simple, mindful practice that extends beyond cooking and influences broader lifestyle choices.

Benefits of Sourdough Discard – Flavor, Nutrition, and Sustainability

Sourdough discard is more than just an ingredient; it is a culinary powerhouse loaded with health benefits and flavor. Unlike other types of discard, which might offer limited applications, sourdough discard adds complexity, depth, and a unique tang to each recipe, thanks to the natural fermentation process. This process breaks down phytic acid, enhancing nutrient absorption in the body. Fermentation also pre-digests some of the flour, making the end product easier on the digestive system—a benefit appreciated by families seeking more wholesome food options.

The flavors imparted by sourdough discard are truly unique. From a subtle tanginess to a deep umami quality in savory applications, discard can transform ordinary recipes into memorable dishes. Its natural acidity enhances other flavors, often allowing recipes to use less added sugar or salt. This quality makes it an appealing option for those looking to prepare healthier, lower-sodium, and lower-sugar meals without sacrificing taste. Sourdough discard also contributes a texture that's hard to replicate; it creates fluffiness in pancakes, chewiness in cookies, and a tender crumb in muffins. This versatility encourages bakers to experiment with a range of culinary applications, from hearty breads to delicate pastries.

Beyond its flavor and nutritional benefits, sourdough discard symbolizes a sustainable choice, aligning with the zero-waste movement that aims to reduce food waste at every stage of production and consumption. Instead of discarding a product that required time, energy, and resources to cultivate, home bakers can find ways to reuse it effectively. This sustainable approach helps families cut down on waste, reinforcing a mindful relationship with food that values each ingredient's potential. In a world where food waste is a growing concern, sourdough discard offers an easy, enjoyable way to be part of the solution while providing delicious, nutritious food for the family.

Essentials for Sourdough Success – Tools, Tips, and Tricks

Achieving success in sourdough baking is as much about the process as it is about the ingredients. Working with sourdough discard requires understanding a few essential tools and techniques to ensure recipes turn out consistently well. Basic tools such as a kitchen scale, a mixing bowl, a sturdy spatula, and airtight jars are essential for handling and storing sourdough discard. Accurate measurements, for example, play a crucial role in ensuring consistency in recipes, particularly when it comes to hydration levels. A digital kitchen scale, therefore, becomes indispensable in any sourdough kitchen, helping to measure ingredients precisely and avoid common pitfalls.

Another important tool is a quality mixing bowl that allows for easy handling of the dough, especially as sourdough discard recipes often require a bit of extra mixing due to their natural hydration. Airtight jars are also essential, as they prevent the discard from drying out and help maintain the starter's ideal condition when stored in the refrigerator. Additionally, for certain recipes, tools like a rolling pin, a bench scraper, and parchment paper can make handling and shaping sourdough discard doughs easier and more efficient.

To enhance success in sourdough baking, it's useful to know a few practical tips. First, allowing discard to reach room temperature before using it in a recipe can enhance its flavor and texture. Cold discard can result in uneven texture and affect the rise of baked goods, while room-temperature discard blends more seamlessly. Second, using discard within a week of its last feeding typically yields the best flavor. Discard that sits too long may become overly sour, which can overpower the intended taste of certain recipes. When managing discard, it's also helpful to label jars with feeding dates, which allows bakers to monitor the starter's age and make informed decisions about its use.

Maintaining and Storing Your Sourdough Discard

Maintaining sourdough discard doesn't require much effort, but a few basic practices can extend its life and maximize its versatility. Since discard is the byproduct of a live culture, proper storage is crucial to maintaining its quality. Ideally, discard should be stored in an airtight container in the refrigerator, where the low temperature slows down fermentation. This method preserves its usability and prevents it from becoming too acidic or overactive, which could interfere with certain recipes. For families who bake often, keeping a larger batch of discard on hand can be convenient, while those who bake occasionally may opt to store smaller quantities to avoid excess.

Bakers can freeze discard for longer storage, typically in portions measured for future recipes. By freezing small amounts in labeled containers or silicone molds, bakers can simply thaw the desired quantity and incorporate it directly into recipes. Frozen discard may slightly alter the texture of baked goods, particularly in recipes that require a light crumb, but it works well for pancakes, waffles, and other items where texture is more forgiving. Defrosted discard should always be allowed to reach room temperature before use, as this ensures the best integration with other ingredients.

The regular maintenance of a sourdough starter directly affects the quality of discard. Feeding the starter consistently results in a healthy, vibrant culture that produces discard with a balanced, mild flavor. However, even discard from less frequently fed starters can be used, though it may be more sour. Bakers who prefer milder flavors can adjust by using fresher discard, while those who enjoy a pronounced tang may opt for older portions.

CHAPTER 1: MORNING DELIGHTS TO START YOUR DAY RIGHT

Apple Cinnamon Morning Muffins

- **Preparation Time**: 15 minutes
- **Cooking Time**: 25 minutes
- **Servings**: 12 muffins

Ingredients

- 1 cup sourdough discard
- 1 1/2 cups all-purpose flour
- 1/2 cup rolled oats
- 1 teaspoon baking powder
- 1/2 teaspoon baking soda
- 1 teaspoon ground cinnamon
- 1/2 teaspoon salt
- 1/2 cup unsweetened applesauce
- 1/2 cup maple syrup or honey
- 1/4 cup melted coconut oil
- 1 teaspoon vanilla extract
- 1 large apple, peeled and diced
- Optional: 1/4 cup chopped walnuts or pecans

Directions

1. Preheat your oven to 375°F (190°C). Line a 12-cup muffin tin with paper liners or lightly grease.
2. In a large mixing bowl, combine the flour, oats, baking powder, baking soda, cinnamon, and salt.
3. In a separate bowl, mix the sourdough discard, applesauce, maple syrup (or honey), melted coconut oil, and vanilla extract until smooth.
4. Add the wet ingredients to the dry ingredients and stir until just combined. Gently fold in the diced apple and nuts (if using).
5. Scoop the batter into the prepared muffin tin, filling each cup about 3/4 full.
6. Bake for 20-25 minutes, or until a toothpick inserted into the center comes out clean.
7. Allow muffins to cool in the pan for 5 minutes, then transfer to a wire rack to cool completely.

Nutritional Values (per muffin)

- Calories: 150
- Protein: 3g
- Carbohydrates: 25g
- Fat: 5g
- Fiber: 2g
- Sugar: 10g

Tips & Tricks

- For extra flavor, add a dash of nutmeg or cloves.
- Store muffins in an airtight container at room temperature for up to 3 days, or freeze for longer storage.
- Use firm apples like Honeycrisp or Granny Smith for the best texture.

Classic Sourdough Bagels

- **Preparation Time**: 20 minutes (plus 1-hour resting time)
- **Cooking Time**: 25 minutes
- **Servings**: 8 bagels

Ingredients

- 1 cup sourdough discard
- 1 1/4 cups warm water
- 3 1/2 cups bread flour
- 1 tablespoon honey
- 1 teaspoon salt
- 1 tablespoon baking soda (for boiling water)

Directions

1. In a mixing bowl, combine the sourdough discard, warm water, flour, honey, and salt. Knead until a smooth dough forms (about 8-10 minutes).
2. Cover the dough with a damp towel and let it rest for 1 hour in a warm place.
3. After resting, divide the dough into 8 equal portions. Roll each portion into a ball, then press your thumb through the center to form a bagel shape.
4. Preheat your oven to 425°F (220°C). Bring a pot of water to a boil and add baking soda.
5. Boil each bagel for 1-2 minutes per side, then transfer to a parchment-lined baking sheet.
6. Bake the bagels for 20-25 minutes, or until golden brown.

Nutritional Values (per bagel)

- Calories: 200
- Protein: 6g
- Carbohydrates: 40g
- Fat: 1g
- Fiber: 2g
- Sugar: 2g

Tips & Tricks

- Add toppings like sesame seeds or poppy seeds before baking for extra flavor.
- Boiling the bagels in baking soda water gives them a chewy crust, a traditional characteristic of bagels.
- Store in an airtight container or freeze for later use.

Banana Nut Bread with a Twist

- **Preparation Time**: 10 minutes
- **Cooking Time**: 55 minutes
- **Servings**: 8 slices

Ingredients

- 1 cup sourdough discard
- 2 ripe bananas, mashed
- 1/4 cup melted butter or coconut oil
- 1/4 cup honey or maple syrup
- 1 large egg
- 1 1/2 cups all-purpose flour
- 1 teaspoon baking powder
- 1/2 teaspoon baking soda
- 1/2 teaspoon salt
- 1/4 teaspoon ground cinnamon
- 1/4 cup chopped walnuts (optional)

Directions

1. Preheat your oven to 350°F (175°C). Grease a 9x5-inch loaf pan.

2. In a large bowl, mix together the sourdough discard, mashed bananas, melted butter, honey, and egg until smooth.

3. In another bowl, whisk the flour, baking powder, baking soda, salt, and cinnamon.

4. Gradually add the dry ingredients to the wet mixture, stirring until just combined. Fold in the walnuts if using.

5. Pour the batter into the prepared loaf pan and smooth the top.

6. Bake for 50-55 minutes, or until a toothpick inserted into the center comes out clean.

7. Allow the bread to cool in the pan for 10 minutes before transferring to a wire rack.

Nutritional Values (per slice)

- Calories: 180
- Protein: 4g
- Carbohydrates: 30g
- Fat: 6g
- Fiber: 2g
- Sugar: 10g

Tips & Tricks

- For added flavor, mix in a tablespoon of chocolate chips or dried cranberries.
- Use overripe bananas for the best texture and sweetness.

Wholesome Breakfast Burritos

- **Preparation Time**: 15 minutes
- **Cooking Time**: 10 minutes
- **Servings**: 4 burritos

Ingredients

- 1 cup sourdough discard
- 4 large flour tortillas
- 4 large eggs, beaten
- 1/2 cup shredded cheddar cheese
- 1/4 cup diced bell pepper
- 1/4 cup diced onion
- 1/4 cup cooked black beans (optional)
- Salt and pepper to taste
- 1 tablespoon olive oil

Directions

1. Heat olive oil in a skillet over medium heat. Add the bell pepper and onion, cooking until softened, about 3 minutes.

2. Add the beaten eggs to the skillet and cook, stirring occasionally, until scrambled.

3. Stir in the sourdough discard, cheese, black beans, salt, and pepper. Cook for an additional 1-2 minutes.

4. Spoon the egg mixture evenly onto each tortilla and roll tightly into burritos.

5. Optional: For a crispy exterior, lightly toast the burritos in a skillet for 1-2 minutes per side before serving.

Nutritional Values (per burrito)

- Calories: 280
- Protein: 12g

- Carbohydrates: 32g
- Fat: 12g
- Fiber: 4g
- Sugar: 2g

Tips & Tricks

- Customize with salsa, avocado, or hot sauce for extra flavor.
- Wrap burritos individually and freeze for quick, reheatable breakfasts.

Lemon Poppy Seed Muffins

- **Preparation Time**: 15 minutes
- **Cooking Time**: 20 minutes
- **Servings**: 12 muffins

Ingredients

- 1 cup sourdough discard
- 1 1/2 cups all-purpose flour
- 1/2 cup granulated sugar
- 1 tablespoon poppy seeds
- 1 teaspoon baking powder
- 1/2 teaspoon baking soda
- 1/4 teaspoon salt
- Zest of 1 lemon
- 1/2 cup plain Greek yogurt
- 1/4 cup melted butter or vegetable oil
- 2 large eggs
- 2 tablespoons fresh lemon juice
- 1 teaspoon vanilla extract

Directions

1. Preheat your oven to 375°F (190°C). Line a 12-cup muffin tin with paper liners or lightly grease.
2. In a large bowl, whisk together flour, sugar, poppy seeds, baking powder, baking soda, salt, and lemon zest.
3. In a separate bowl, combine the sourdough discard, Greek yogurt, melted butter, eggs, lemon juice, and vanilla extract.
4. Pour the wet ingredients into the dry ingredients, stirring until just combined.
5. Divide the batter evenly among the muffin cups, filling each about 3/4 full.
6. Bake for 18-20 minutes, or until a toothpick inserted into the center comes out clean.
7. Let muffins cool in the pan for 5 minutes before transferring to a wire rack.

Nutritional Values (per muffin)

- Calories: 160
- Protein: 4g
- Carbohydrates: 24g
- Fat: 6g
- Fiber: 1g
- Sugar: 9g

Tips & Tricks

- For a stronger lemon flavor, add a bit more lemon zest.
- These muffins freeze well; just thaw at room temperature when ready to eat.

Cornbread Pancakes

- **Preparation Time**: 10 minutes
- **Cooking Time**: 15 minutes
- **Servings**: 4 (makes 8 small pancakes)

Ingredients

- 1/2 cup sourdough discard
- 1/2 cup cornmeal
- 1/2 cup all-purpose flour
- 1 tablespoon sugar
- 1 teaspoon baking powder
- 1/2 teaspoon salt
- 3/4 cup milk
- 1 large egg
- 2 tablespoons melted butter

Directions

1. In a large bowl, whisk together cornmeal, flour, sugar, baking powder, and salt.
2. In another bowl, combine the sourdough discard, milk, egg, and melted butter.
3. Add the wet ingredients to the dry ingredients, mixing until just combined.
4. Heat a nonstick skillet over medium heat and lightly grease.
5. Pour 1/4 cup batter onto the skillet for each pancake, cooking for 2-3 minutes per side until golden brown.
6. Serve warm with maple syrup or honey.

Nutritional Values (per pancake)

- Calories: 80
- Protein: 2g
- Carbohydrates: 12g
- Fat: 3g
- Fiber: 1g
- Sugar: 1g

Tips & Tricks

- Add a handful of fresh corn kernels to the batter for added texture.
- To make savory cornbread pancakes, mix in chopped jalapenos or shredded cheese.

Sourdough Spinach Quiche

- **Preparation Time**: 15 minutes
- **Cooking Time**: 30 minutes
- **Servings**: 6

Ingredients

- 1 cup sourdough discard
- 1 pre-made pie crust (or homemade if preferred)
- 1 cup fresh spinach, chopped
- 1/2 cup shredded cheddar cheese
- 4 large eggs
- 1/2 cup milk
- 1/2 teaspoon salt
- 1/4 teaspoon black pepper
- 1/4 teaspoon nutmeg

Directions

1. Preheat your oven to 350°F (175°C). Place the pie crust in a pie dish and set aside.
2. In a large bowl, whisk together the eggs, milk, salt, pepper, and nutmeg.
3. Stir in the sourdough discard, spinach, and cheese.
4. Pour the filling into the pie crust.
5. Bake for 30-35 minutes, or until the center is set.
6. Let the quiche cool for a few minutes before slicing and serving.

Nutritional Values (per slice)

- Calories: 180
- Protein: 8g
- Carbohydrates: 12g
- Fat: 11g
- Fiber: 1g
- Sugar: 1g

Tips & Tricks

- Substitute other greens like kale or arugula for the spinach.
- Serve warm or at room temperature; leftovers can be refrigerated for up to 3 days.

Fluffy Discard Pancakes

- **Preparation Time**: 5 minutes
- **Cooking Time**: 15 minutes
- **Servings**: 4 (makes about 8 pancakes)

Ingredients

- 1 cup sourdough discard
- 1 cup all-purpose flour
- 1 tablespoon sugar
- 1 teaspoon baking powder
- 1/2 teaspoon baking soda
- 1/4 teaspoon salt
- 3/4 cup milk
- 1 large egg
- 2 tablespoons melted butter

Directions

1. In a large bowl, whisk together flour, sugar, baking powder, baking soda, and salt.
2. In a separate bowl, mix the sourdough discard, milk, egg, and melted butter.
3. Pour the wet ingredients into the dry ingredients, stirring until just combined.
4. Heat a nonstick skillet over medium heat and lightly grease.
5. Pour 1/4 cup of batter onto the skillet for each pancake and cook for 2-3 minutes per side.
6. Serve warm with your favorite toppings.

Nutritional Values (per pancake)

- Calories: 90
- Protein: 3g
- Carbohydrates: 14g
- Fat: 3g
- Fiber: 1g
- Sugar: 2g

Tips & Tricks

- For extra fluffiness, let the batter rest for 5-10 minutes before cooking.
- Add blueberries or chocolate chips for a twist on classic pancakes.

Warm Cinnamon Rolls

- **Preparation Time**: 25 minutes (plus 1-hour resting time)
- **Cooking Time**: 25 minutes
- **Servings**: 12 rolls

Ingredients

Dough

- 1 cup sourdough discard
- 3 cups all-purpose flour
- 1/4 cup granulated sugar
- 1 teaspoon salt
- 1/4 cup unsalted butter, melted
- 1 large egg
- 1/2 cup warm milk

Filling

- 1/4 cup unsalted butter, softened
- 1/2 cup brown sugar
- 1 tablespoon ground cinnamon

Glaze

- 1 cup powdered sugar
- 1-2 tablespoons milk or cream
- 1/2 teaspoon vanilla extract

Directions

1. In a large mixing bowl, combine the sourdough discard, flour, sugar, salt, melted butter, egg, and warm milk. Knead until a soft, smooth dough forms (about 8-10 minutes).
2. Cover the dough and let it rest for 1 hour in a warm place.
3. Roll out the dough on a floured surface into a rectangle, about 1/4 inch thick.
4. Spread the softened butter over the dough, then sprinkle the brown sugar and cinnamon evenly on top.
5. Roll the dough tightly into a log and cut into 12 equal rolls. Place the rolls in a greased baking dish.
6. Preheat your oven to 350°F (175°C) and bake the rolls for 20-25 minutes or until golden brown.
7. For the glaze, mix powdered sugar, milk, and vanilla extract until smooth, then drizzle over the warm rolls.

Nutritional Values (per roll)

- Calories: 220
- Protein: 4g
- Carbohydrates: 34g
- Fat: 7g
- Fiber: 1g
- Sugar: 14g

Tips & Tricks

- For softer rolls, cover with foil halfway through baking.
- Add chopped nuts or raisins to the filling for extra texture.

Zucchini Morning Loaf

- **Preparation Time**: 15 minutes
- **Cooking Time**: 50 minutes
- **Servings**: 8 slices

Ingredients

- 1 cup sourdough discard
- 1 1/2 cups grated zucchini (squeezed dry)
- 1 1/2 cups all-purpose flour
- 1/2 cup granulated sugar
- 1/4 cup melted coconut oil
- 1 teaspoon baking powder
- 1/2 teaspoon baking soda
- 1/2 teaspoon salt
- 1 teaspoon ground cinnamon
- 1/4 teaspoon ground nutmeg
- 1/2 cup chopped walnuts or chocolate chips (optional)

Directions

1. Preheat your oven to 350°F (175°C). Grease a 9x5-inch loaf pan.
2. In a large bowl, combine flour, sugar, baking powder, baking soda, salt, cinnamon, and nutmeg.
3. In a separate bowl, mix the sourdough discard, grated zucchini, and melted coconut oil.
4. Pour the wet ingredients into the dry ingredients and stir until just combined. Fold in walnuts or chocolate chips if desired.
5. Pour the batter into the prepared loaf pan and bake for 50-55 minutes.
6. Cool in the pan for 10 minutes, then transfer to a wire rack to finish cooling.

Nutritional Values (per slice)

- Calories: 180
- Protein: 3g
- Carbohydrates: 28g
- Fat: 7g
- Fiber: 2g
- Sugar: 10g

Tips & Tricks

- Squeeze the zucchini well to prevent excess moisture.
- Add a sprinkle of shredded coconut for a tropical twist.

Dutch Baby with Berries

- **Preparation Time**: 10 minutes
- **Cooking Time**: 20 minutes
- **Servings**: 4

Ingredients

- 1/2 cup sourdough discard
- 1/2 cup all-purpose flour
- 1/2 cup milk
- 3 large eggs
- 1 tablespoon sugar
- 1/2 teaspoon vanilla extract
- 2 tablespoons unsalted butter

- Fresh berries and powdered sugar for serving

Directions

1. Preheat your oven to 425°F (220°C). Place a cast-iron skillet in the oven to heat.
2. In a blender, combine sourdough discard, flour, milk, eggs, sugar, and vanilla. Blend until smooth.
3. Carefully remove the hot skillet from the oven and add the butter, swirling to coat.
4. Pour the batter into the skillet and bake for 20 minutes or until puffed and golden.
5. Serve warm with fresh berries and a dusting of powdered sugar.

Nutritional Values (per serving)

- Calories: 180
- Protein: 6g
- Carbohydrates: 20g
- Fat: 8g
- Fiber: 1g
- Sugar: 5g

Tips & Tricks

- This batter can be made ahead of time and refrigerated overnight.
- Use seasonal fruits to vary the toppings throughout the year.

Morning Glory Muffins

- **Preparation Time**: 15 minutes
- **Cooking Time**: 25 minutes
- **Servings**: 12 muffins

Ingredients

- 1 cup sourdough discard
- 1 1/2 cups all-purpose flour
- 1/2 cup rolled oats
- 1/2 cup grated carrot
- 1/2 cup grated apple
- 1/4 cup raisins
- 1/2 cup granulated sugar
- 1 teaspoon baking powder
- 1/2 teaspoon baking soda
- 1/2 teaspoon salt
- 1 teaspoon ground cinnamon
- 1/2 cup melted coconut oil
- 1/4 cup chopped nuts (optional)

Directions

1. Preheat your oven to 375°F (190°C). Line a 12-cup muffin tin with paper liners.
2. In a large bowl, combine flour, oats, sugar, baking powder, baking soda, salt, and cinnamon.
3. In a separate bowl, mix the sourdough discard, melted coconut oil, grated carrot, grated apple, and raisins.
4. Add the wet ingredients to the dry ingredients and mix until just combined. Fold in the nuts if desired.
5. Divide the batter among the muffin cups and bake for 20-25 minutes.
6. Cool in the pan for a few minutes, then transfer to a wire rack.

Nutritional Values (per muffin)

- Calories: 200
- Protein: 4g
- Carbohydrates: 30g
- Fat: 8g
- Fiber: 3g
- Sugar: 12g

Tips & Tricks

- These muffins freeze well; reheat in the microwave for a quick breakfast.
- Add 1 tablespoon of chia seeds for an extra fiber boost.

Breakfast Casserole

- **Preparation Time**: 15 minutes
- **Cooking Time**: 40 minutes
- **Servings**: 6

Ingredients

- 1 cup sourdough discard
- 6 large eggs
- 1/2 cup milk
- 1 cup cooked sausage or bacon, crumbled
- 1 cup shredded cheddar cheese
- 1/2 cup diced bell pepper
- 1/2 cup diced onion
- Salt and pepper to taste
- 1 tablespoon olive oil (for greasing)

Directions

1. Preheat your oven to 350°F (175°C). Lightly grease a 9x13-inch baking dish with olive oil.
2. In a large bowl, whisk together eggs, milk, sourdough discard, salt, and pepper.
3. Add the sausage, cheese, bell pepper, and onion to the egg mixture, stirring to combine.
4. Pour the mixture into the prepared baking dish.
5. Bake for 35-40 minutes, or until the center is set and the edges are golden brown.
6. Allow the casserole to cool for 5 minutes before slicing and serving.

Nutritional Values (per serving)

- Calories: 250
- Protein: 15g
- Carbohydrates: 6g
- Fat: 18g
- Fiber: 1g
- Sugar: 2g

Tips & Tricks

- Substitute vegetables like spinach or mushrooms for additional flavor.
- This casserole can be made a day in advance and reheated in the oven before serving.

Sourdough Pop-Tarts

- **Preparation Time**: 30 minutes
- **Cooking Time**: 25 minutes

- **Servings**: 6 pop-tarts

Ingredients

Dough

- 1 cup sourdough discard
- 2 cups all-purpose flour
- 1 tablespoon sugar
- 1/2 teaspoon salt
- 1/2 cup unsalted butter, cold and cubed
- 1/4 cup ice water

Filling

- 1/2 cup fruit jam or preserves of choice

Glaze

- 1/2 cup powdered sugar
- 1-2 tablespoons milk
- 1/4 teaspoon vanilla extract

Directions

1. In a mixing bowl, combine flour, sugar, and salt. Cut in the butter until the mixture resembles coarse crumbs.
2. Stir in the sourdough discard and ice water, mixing until a dough forms. Wrap and chill for 30 minutes.
3. Preheat oven to 375°F (190°C). Roll out the dough to 1/8-inch thickness and cut into rectangles.
4. Place 1 tablespoon of jam on half of the rectangles, then top with the remaining dough rectangles. Press edges with a fork to seal.
5. Place on a baking sheet lined with parchment and bake for 20-25 minutes.
6. Mix glaze ingredients and drizzle over cooled pop-tarts.

Nutritional Values (per pop-tart)

- Calories: 220
- Protein: 3g
- Carbohydrates: 30g
- Fat: 10g
- Fiber: 1g
- Sugar: 10g

Tips & Tricks

- Use any type of jam or fruit filling to customize the flavor.
- Store pop-tarts in an airtight container for up to 3 days.

Blueberry Oat Bars

- **Preparation Time**: 15 minutes
- **Cooking Time**: 30 minutes
- **Servings**: 9 bars

Ingredients

- 1 cup sourdough discard
- 1 cup rolled oats
- 1/2 cup all-purpose flour
- 1/2 cup brown sugar
- 1/2 teaspoon baking soda
- 1/4 teaspoon salt
- 1/2 cup unsalted butter, melted
- 1 cup fresh or frozen blueberries
- 1 tablespoon honey

Directions

1. Preheat your oven to 350°F (175°C). Grease an 8x8-inch baking pan.
2. In a large bowl, combine oats, flour, brown sugar, baking soda, and salt.
3. Add the sourdough discard and melted butter, mixing until the mixture forms coarse crumbs.
4. Press half of the oat mixture into the prepared pan.
5. In a small bowl, toss blueberries with honey and spread over the oat layer.
6. Sprinkle the remaining oat mixture over the blueberries.
7. Bake for 25-30 minutes or until golden brown. Let cool before cutting.

Nutritional Values (per bar)

- Calories: 180
- Protein: 3g
- Carbohydrates: 28g
- Fat: 7g
- Fiber: 2g
- Sugar: 12g

Tips & Tricks

- Substitute other berries, such as raspberries or strawberries, if preferred.
- Bars can be refrigerated for up to a week for easy grab-and-go snacks.

Savory Waffles

- **Preparation Time**: 10 minutes
- **Cooking Time**: 15 minutes
- **Servings**: 4 waffles

Ingredients

- 1 cup sourdough discard
- 1 cup all-purpose flour
- 1 teaspoon baking powder
- 1/2 teaspoon baking soda
- 1/4 teaspoon salt
- 3/4 cup milk
- 1 large egg
- 1/4 cup shredded cheddar cheese
- 2 tablespoons chopped chives
- 2 tablespoons melted butter

Directions

1. Preheat your waffle iron and grease if necessary.
2. In a large bowl, whisk together flour, baking powder, baking soda, and salt.
3. In another bowl, mix sourdough discard, milk, egg, melted butter, cheese, and chives.
4. Add the wet ingredients to the dry ingredients and stir until just combined.
5. Pour the batter into the waffle iron and cook according to the manufacturer's instructions.
6. Serve warm with butter or a savory topping.

Nutritional Values (per waffle)

- Calories: 200
- Protein: 6g
- Carbohydrates: 25g
- Fat: 8g

- Fiber: 1g
- Sugar: 2g

Tips & Tricks

- For added flavor, mix in cooked, crumbled bacon.
- Waffles freeze well; just toast them for a quick breakfast.

Nutty Cereal Bars

- **Preparation Time**: 10 minutes
- **Cooking Time**: 20 minutes
- **Servings**: 12 bars

Ingredients

- 1 cup sourdough discard
- 1/2 cup rolled oats
- 1/2 cup chopped almonds
- 1/2 cup peanut butter
- 1/4 cup honey or maple syrup
- 1/2 teaspoon vanilla extract
- 1/4 teaspoon salt

Directions

1. Preheat your oven to 350°F (175°C). Line an 8x8-inch baking pan with parchment.
2. In a large bowl, mix sourdough discard, oats, almonds, peanut butter, honey, vanilla, and salt until well combined.
3. Press the mixture into the prepared baking pan.
4. Bake for 20 minutes or until golden brown.
5. Let cool before cutting into bars.

Nutritional Values (per bar)

- Calories: 150
- Protein: 4g
- Carbohydrates: 14g
- Fat: 8g
- Fiber: 2g
- Sugar: 7g

Tips & Tricks

- Substitute almonds with other nuts or seeds as preferred.
- Wrap bars individually for a convenient snack on the go.

French Toast Loaf

- **Preparation Time**: 10 minutes
- **Cooking Time**: 25 minutes
- **Servings**: 6 slices

Ingredients

- 1 cup sourdough discard
- 6 slices of day-old bread
- 4 large eggs
- 1/2 cup milk
- 1 tablespoon maple syrup
- 1 teaspoon vanilla extract
- 1/2 teaspoon cinnamon

Directions

1. Preheat your oven to 350°F (175°C). Lightly grease a baking dish.

2. In a large bowl, whisk together eggs, milk, sourdough discard, maple syrup, vanilla, and cinnamon.
3. Dip each slice of bread into the mixture and arrange in the baking dish.
4. Pour any remaining mixture over the top.
5. Bake for 25 minutes or until golden brown.
6. Serve warm with additional syrup if desired.

Nutritional Values (per slice)

- Calories: 150
- Protein: 6g
- Carbohydrates: 18g
- Fat: 6g
- Fiber: 1g
- Sugar: 5g

Tips & Tricks

- Use a sturdy bread like brioche or challah for the best texture.
- Add sliced bananas or berries between the layers for extra flavor.

Pumpkin Spice Scones

- **Preparation Time**: 15 minutes
- **Cooking Time**: 20 minutes
- **Servings**: 8 scones

Ingredients

- 1 cup sourdough discard
- 2 cups all-purpose flour
- 1/4 cup brown sugar
- 1 tablespoon baking powder
- 1/2 teaspoon baking soda
- 1 teaspoon ground cinnamon
- 1/2 teaspoon ground nutmeg
- 1/2 teaspoon ground ginger
- 1/2 teaspoon salt
- 1/2 cup cold unsalted butter, cubed
- 1/2 cup canned pumpkin puree
- 1 teaspoon vanilla extract

Directions

1. Preheat your oven to 400°F (200°C). Line a baking sheet with parchment paper.
2. In a large bowl, mix together flour, brown sugar, baking powder, baking soda, cinnamon, nutmeg, ginger, and salt.
3. Cut in the cold butter until the mixture resembles coarse crumbs.
4. In a separate bowl, combine the sourdough discard, pumpkin puree, and vanilla extract.
5. Add the wet mixture to the dry ingredients and mix until just combined.
6. Turn the dough out onto a floured surface, pat it into a circle about 1 inch thick, and cut into 8 wedges.
7. Place scones on the prepared baking sheet and bake for 18-20 minutes until golden brown.

Nutritional Values (per scone)

- Calories: 230
- Protein: 4g
- Carbohydrates: 32g
- Fat: 9g
- Fiber: 2g
- Sugar: 8g

Tips & Tricks

- For added flavor, drizzle with a simple vanilla glaze.
- These scones freeze well; reheat in the oven for a quick breakfast treat.

Frittata with Sourdough Base

- **Preparation Time**: 10 minutes
- **Cooking Time**: 30 minutes
- **Servings**: 6

Ingredients

- 1 cup sourdough discard
- 6 large eggs
- 1/2 cup milk
- 1 cup diced bell peppers
- 1/2 cup sliced mushrooms
- 1/2 cup shredded cheese
- Salt and pepper to taste
- 1 tablespoon olive oil

Directions

1. Preheat your oven to 350°F (175°C).
2. In a mixing bowl, whisk together eggs, milk, sourdough discard, salt, and pepper.
3. Heat olive oil in an oven-safe skillet over medium heat. Add bell peppers and mushrooms, cooking until softened.
4. Pour the egg mixture into the skillet and sprinkle with cheese.
5. Transfer to the oven and bake for 25-30 minutes or until the center is set.
6. Slice and serve warm.

Nutritional Values (per serving)

- Calories: 180
- Protein: 10g
- Carbohydrates: 4g
- Fat: 12g
- Fiber: 1g
- Sugar: 2g

Tips & Tricks

- Customize with any vegetables or herbs you prefer.
- Leftovers make a great sandwich filling when cold.

Chocolate Chip Muffins

- **Preparation Time**: 10 minutes
- **Cooking Time**: 20 minutes
- **Servings**: 12 muffins

Ingredients

- 1 cup sourdough discard
- 1 1/2 cups all-purpose flour
- 1/2 cup sugar
- 1 teaspoon baking powder

- 1/2 teaspoon baking soda
- 1/2 teaspoon salt
- 1/2 cup milk
- 1/3 cup melted butter
- 1 large egg
- 1 cup chocolate chips

Directions

1. Preheat your oven to 375°F (190°C). Line a 12-cup muffin tin with paper liners.
2. In a large bowl, whisk together flour, sugar, baking powder, baking soda, and salt.
3. In a separate bowl, mix sourdough discard, milk, melted butter, and egg.
4. Pour the wet ingredients into the dry ingredients and stir until just combined. Fold in chocolate chips.
5. Divide the batter among muffin cups and bake for 18-20 minutes until golden.
6. Cool in the pan for a few minutes, then transfer to a wire rack.

Nutritional Values (per muffin)

- Calories: 210
- Protein: 4g
- Carbohydrates: 30g
- Fat: 9g
- Fiber: 1g
- Sugar: 15g

Tips & Tricks

- For a flavor twist, add a teaspoon of orange zest.
- Muffins freeze well; reheat briefly in the microwave before serving.

Cheese and Herb Breakfast Biscuits

- **Preparation Time**: 15 minutes
- **Cooking Time**: 15 minutes
- **Servings**: 12 biscuits

Ingredients

- 1 cup sourdough discard
- 2 cups all-purpose flour
- 1 tablespoon baking powder
- 1/2 teaspoon salt
- 1/2 cup cold unsalted butter, cubed
- 1/2 cup shredded cheddar cheese
- 1 tablespoon chopped fresh chives
- 3/4 cup milk

Directions

1. Preheat your oven to 425°F (220°C). Line a baking sheet with parchment paper.
2. In a large bowl, mix flour, baking powder, and salt.
3. Cut in the cold butter until the mixture resembles coarse crumbs.
4. Add sourdough discard, cheese, chives, and milk, stirring until just combined.
5. Turn the dough onto a floured surface, pat to about 1 inch thick, and cut with a biscuit cutter.

6. Place biscuits on the baking sheet and bake for 12-15 minutes until golden.

Nutritional Values (per biscuit)

- Calories: 180
- Protein: 4g
- Carbohydrates: 22g
- Fat: 8g
- Fiber: 1g
- Sugar: 1g

Tips & Tricks

- Substitute cheddar with other cheeses like gruyere or parmesan.
- These biscuits are perfect for breakfast sandwiches.

Breakfast Cookies with Nuts

- **Preparation Time**: 10 minutes
- **Cooking Time**: 12 minutes
- **Servings**: 12 cookies

Ingredients

- 1 cup sourdough discard
- 1 1/2 cups rolled oats
- 1/2 cup almond flour
- 1/4 cup honey or maple syrup
- 1/4 cup chopped walnuts or almonds
- 1/4 cup dried cranberries
- 1 teaspoon vanilla extract
- 1/2 teaspoon cinnamon
- 1/4 teaspoon salt

Directions

1. Preheat your oven to 350°F (175°C). Line a baking sheet with parchment paper.
2. In a large bowl, combine oats, almond flour, nuts, cranberries, cinnamon, and salt.
3. Stir in the sourdough discard, honey, and vanilla extract until well combined.
4. Drop spoonfuls of dough onto the baking sheet and flatten slightly.
5. Bake for 10-12 minutes or until edges are golden.
6. Cool on a wire rack.

Nutritional Values (per cookie)

- Calories: 140
- Protein: 3g
- Carbohydrates: 18g
- Fat: 6g
- Fiber: 2g
- Sugar: 6g

Tips & Tricks

- For a flavor boost, add a pinch of nutmeg or ginger.
- Store in an airtight container for up to a week.

Sourdough Crepes

- **Preparation Time**: 5 minutes (plus 30 minutes resting time)
- **Cooking Time**: 20 minutes
- **Servings**: 12 crepes

Ingredients

- 1 cup sourdough discard
- 1/2 cup all-purpose flour
- 1/2 cup milk
- 1/2 cup water
- 2 large eggs
- 2 tablespoons melted butter
- Pinch of salt

Directions

1. In a blender, combine sourdough discard, flour, milk, water, eggs, melted butter, and salt. Blend until smooth.
2. Let the batter rest for 30 minutes in the refrigerator.
3. Heat a nonstick skillet over medium heat and lightly grease with butter.
4. Pour 1/4 cup batter into the skillet, swirling to coat the bottom in a thin layer.
5. Cook for 1-2 minutes per side or until golden. Repeat with remaining batter.
6. Serve with desired fillings or toppings.

Nutritional Values (per crepe)

- Calories: 70
- Protein: 2g
- Carbohydrates: 8g
- Fat: 3g
- Fiber: 0g
- Sugar: 1g

Tips & Tricks

- Crepes can be made in advance and stored in the refrigerator.
- Try fillings like fresh fruit, nut butter, or a sprinkle of powdered sugar.

Sourdough Crepes

- **Preparation Time**: 5 minutes (plus 30 minutes resting time)
- **Cooking Time**: 20 minutes
- **Servings**: 12 crepes

Ingredients

- 1 cup sourdough discard
- 1/2 cup all-purpose flour
- 1/2 cup milk
- 1/2 cup water
- 2 large eggs
- 2 tablespoons melted butter
- Pinch of salt

Directions

1. In a blender, combine sourdough discard, flour, milk, water, eggs, melted butter, and salt. Blend until smooth.
2. Let the batter rest for 30 minutes in the refrigerator.
3. Heat a nonstick skillet over medium heat and lightly grease with butter.
4. Pour 1/4 cup batter into the skillet, swirling to coat the bottom in a thin layer.
5. Cook for 1-2 minutes per side or until golden. Repeat with remaining batter.
6. Serve with desired fillings or toppings.

Nutritional Values (per crepe)

- Calories: 70
- Protein: 2g
- Carbohydrates: 8g
- Fat: 3g
- Fiber: 0g
- Sugar: 1g

Tips & Tricks

- Crepes can be made in advance and stored in the refrigerator.
- Try fillings like fresh fruit, nut butter, or a sprinkle of powdered sugar.

CHAPTER 2: ARTISAN BREADS & SAVORY ROLLS

Everyday Sourdough Loaf

- **Preparation Time:** 20 minutes (plus 4-6 hours rising time)
- **Cooking Time:** 30 minutes
- **Servings:** 1 loaf (approx. 12 slices)

Ingredients:

- 1 cup sourdough discard
- 4 cups all-purpose flour
- 1 ½ cups warm water
- 1 ½ tsp salt
- 1 tsp honey (optional, for added sweetness and color)

Directions:

1. In a large mixing bowl, combine the sourdough discard and warm water. Stir well until fully incorporated.
2. Gradually add the flour, 1 cup at a time, mixing thoroughly after each addition. Add salt and honey (if using).
3. Knead the dough for about 10 minutes until it becomes smooth and elastic. Cover the bowl with a damp cloth and let it rest in a warm place for 4-6 hours, or until it doubles in size.
4. Preheat the oven to 450°F (230°C). Place a Dutch oven or heavy baking pot inside to heat up.
5. Transfer the dough onto a lightly floured surface, shaping it into a round loaf. Carefully place it in the hot Dutch oven, cover, and bake for 20 minutes.
6. Remove the lid and bake for an additional 10-15 minutes, or until the crust is golden brown.
7. Let cool before slicing.

Nutritional Values (per slice):

- Calories: 120
- Carbohydrates: 22g
- Protein: 4g
- Fat: 0.5g
- Fiber: 1g

Tips & Tricks:

- **For a crustier loaf,** place a small dish of water in the oven to create steam.
- **Storage:** Wrap in a cloth bag for up to 3 days at room temperature, or freeze for longer storage.

Seeded Multigrain Bread

- **Preparation Time:** 25 minutes (plus 4-6 hours rising time)
- **Cooking Time:** 35 minutes
- **Servings:** 1 loaf (approx. 12 slices)

Ingredients:

- 1 cup sourdough discard
- 3 cups whole wheat flour
- 1 cup rye flour
- 1 ½ cups warm water
- 1 tbsp honey
- 1 tbsp flax seeds
- 1 tbsp sunflower seeds

- 1 tbsp sesame seeds
- 1 ½ tsp salt

Directions:

1. In a large bowl, combine the sourdough discard, warm water, and honey. Stir well.
2. Gradually add the whole wheat and rye flours, followed by salt and seeds (reserving a small amount of seeds for topping).
3. Knead the dough for 10 minutes until it is smooth. Cover and let rise for 4-6 hours in a warm spot.
4. Preheat the oven to 425°F (220°C). Shape the dough into a loaf and sprinkle the reserved seeds on top.
5. Place on a baking sheet or in a loaf pan and bake for 35 minutes, or until the crust is firm and golden.
6. Let cool before slicing.

Nutritional Values (per slice):

- Calories: 140
- Carbohydrates: 24g
- Protein: 5g
- Fat: 2g
- Fiber: 3g

Tips & Tricks:

- **For an extra nutty flavor,** lightly toast the seeds before adding them to the dough.
- **Storing Tips:** Wrap tightly in plastic wrap and store at room temperature for up to 3 days.

Olive Herb Focaccia

- **Preparation Time:** 15 minutes (plus 3 hours rising time)
- **Cooking Time:** 25 minutes
- **Servings:** 1 focaccia (approx. 12 squares)

Ingredients:

- 1 cup sourdough discard
- 3 cups all-purpose flour
- 1 ¼ cups warm water
- 2 tbsp olive oil, plus extra for drizzling
- 1 tsp salt
- 1 tbsp chopped fresh rosemary
- ½ cup pitted black olives, sliced

Directions:

1. In a bowl, mix the sourdough discard, warm water, and olive oil until well combined.
2. Gradually add the flour and salt, kneading until the dough is soft and slightly sticky.
3. Cover and let the dough rise for 3 hours in a warm place.
4. Preheat oven to 400°F (200°C). Grease a baking sheet with olive oil and stretch the dough onto it.
5. Press olive slices and rosemary into the dough. Drizzle with extra olive oil and sprinkle with a pinch of salt.
6. Bake for 20-25 minutes, or until golden and crisp.
7. Allow to cool slightly before cutting into squares.

Nutritional Values (per square):

- Calories: 130
- Carbohydrates: 20g
- Protein: 3g
- Fat: 4g
- Fiber: 1g

Tips & Tricks:

- **For a softer focaccia,** cover the pan with foil for the first 10 minutes of baking.
- **Serving Suggestion:** Serve with a side of marinara or olive oil and balsamic for dipping.

Classic French Baguettes

- **Preparation Time:** 20 minutes (plus 4 hours rising time)
- **Cooking Time:** 25 minutes
- **Servings:** 2 baguettes (approx. 12 slices per baguette)

Ingredients:

- 1 cup sourdough discard
- 3 ½ cups bread flour
- 1 ½ cups warm water
- 1 tsp salt

Directions:

1. In a large bowl, combine sourdough discard and warm water, stirring until well mixed.
2. Gradually add the flour and salt, kneading until the dough is smooth and elastic.
3. Cover and let rise for 2 hours, then fold the dough and let rise for another 2 hours.
4. Preheat oven to 475°F (245°C). Shape the dough into two long baguettes and place on a baking sheet.
5. Score the top with a sharp knife and bake for 20-25 minutes until golden brown.
6. Allow to cool on a wire rack before slicing.

Nutritional Values (per slice):

- Calories: 90
- Carbohydrates: 18g
- Protein: 3g
- Fat: 0.5g
- Fiber: 1g

Tips & Tricks:

- **For a crispier crust,** mist the baguettes with water before baking.
- **Serving Suggestion:** Enjoy with butter or as the base for bruschetta.

Jalapeño Cheddar Bread

- **Preparation Time:** 25 minutes (plus 3 hours rising time)
- **Cooking Time:** 30 minutes
- **Servings:** 1 loaf (approx. 10 slices)

Ingredients:

- 1 cup sourdough discard
- 3 cups all-purpose flour
- 1 cup warm water

- 1 cup shredded cheddar cheese
- 2-3 jalapeños, sliced thinly
- 1 ½ tsp salt

Directions:

1. In a bowl, combine sourdough discard and warm water, stirring until smooth.
2. Add flour, salt, cheese, and jalapeño slices, mixing until incorporated.
3. Knead for 10 minutes until the dough is smooth and stretchy. Let rise for 3 hours.
4. Preheat oven to 425°F (220°C). Shape dough into a round loaf and place on a baking sheet.
5. Bake for 30 minutes until the top is golden and the cheese is bubbling.
6. Let cool before slicing.

Nutritional Values (per slice):

- Calories: 180
- Carbohydrates: 25g
- Protein: 6g
- Fat: 5g
- Fiber: 1g

Tips & Tricks:

- **For extra spice,** add chopped jalapeño seeds to the dough.
- **Storage Tip:** Wrap tightly in foil and store at room temperature for up to 3 days.

Sweet Potato Dinner Rolls

- **Preparation Time:** 30 minutes (plus 2 hours rising time)
- **Cooking Time:** 20 minutes
- **Servings:** 12 rolls

Ingredients:

- 1 cup sourdough discard
- 3 cups all-purpose flour
- 1 cup mashed sweet potato
- ½ cup warm milk
- 3 tbsp sugar
- 2 tbsp butter, melted
- 1 tsp salt

Directions:

1. In a large bowl, mix sourdough discard, mashed sweet potato, warm milk, and sugar until well combined.
2. Gradually add flour, salt, and melted butter, kneading until smooth.
3. Cover and let rise in a warm place for 2 hours.
4. Preheat oven to 375°F (190°C). Divide dough into 12 rolls and place on a greased baking sheet.
5. Bake for 18-20 minutes or until golden brown.
6. Let cool slightly before serving.

Nutritional Values (per roll):

- Calories: 140
- Carbohydrates: 26g
- Protein: 3g

- Fat: 3g
- Fiber: 1g

Tips & Tricks:

- **Serving Tip:** Brush the tops with melted butter after baking for added flavor.
- **Make Ahead:** These rolls can be made a day in advance and stored in an airtight container.

Soft and Chewy Brioche

- **Preparation Time:** 30 minutes (plus 3 hours rising time)
- **Cooking Time:** 25 minutes
- **Servings:** 1 loaf (approx. 12 slices)

Ingredients:

- 1 cup sourdough discard
- 3 cups bread flour
- ½ cup butter, softened
- ¼ cup sugar
- 3 large eggs
- 1 tsp salt

Directions:

1. In a mixing bowl, combine sourdough discard, sugar, eggs, and salt.
2. Gradually add flour and softened butter, kneading until smooth and elastic.
3. Cover and let rise for 2 hours, then fold the dough and let rise for another hour.
4. Preheat oven to 375°F (190°C). Shape the dough into a loaf or individual rolls.
5. Bake for 25-30 minutes until golden.
6. Let cool on a wire rack before slicing.

Nutritional Values (per slice):

- Calories: 200
- Carbohydrates: 28g
- Protein: 5g
- Fat: 7g
- Fiber: 1g

Tips & Tricks:

- **For extra flavor,** add a splash of vanilla extract to the dough.
- **Storage Tip:** Brioche can be stored at room temperature for up to 2 days or frozen for longer storage.

Savory Spinach Dip Bread Bowl

- **Preparation Time:** 25 minutes (plus 2 hours rising time)
- **Cooking Time:** 30 minutes
- **Servings:** 1 bread bowl (serves 6-8 as an appetizer)

Ingredients:

- 1 cup sourdough discard
- 3 cups all-purpose flour
- 1 ¼ cups warm water
- 1 tsp salt
- 1 cup prepared spinach dip (for serving)

Directions:

1. In a mixing bowl, combine sourdough discard, warm water, and salt. Gradually add flour and knead until a smooth dough forms.
2. Cover and let rise in a warm place for 2 hours or until doubled in size.
3. Preheat oven to 400°F (200°C). Shape the dough into a round loaf and place on a baking sheet.
4. Bake for 25-30 minutes, or until golden brown. Cool slightly.
5. Cut a circular opening in the top, hollow out the bread, and fill with spinach dip.

Nutritional Values (per serving):

- Calories: 180
- Carbohydrates: 32g
- Protein: 5g
- Fat: 2g
- Fiber: 1g

Tips & Tricks:

- **Serving Tip:** Use the removed bread pieces as dippers.
- **Make Ahead:** The bread bowl can be baked the day before and stored in a sealed container.

Pumpernickel Bread

- **Preparation Time:** 30 minutes (plus 3 hours rising time)
- **Cooking Time:** 35 minutes
- **Servings:** 1 loaf (approx. 10 slices)

Ingredients:

- 1 cup sourdough discard
- 2 cups rye flour
- 1 ½ cups all-purpose flour
- 1 cup warm water
- ¼ cup molasses
- 1 tbsp cocoa powder
- 1 tsp salt

Directions:

1. In a mixing bowl, combine sourdough discard, warm water, and molasses.
2. Add rye flour, all-purpose flour, cocoa powder, and salt, mixing until smooth. Knead for 10 minutes.
3. Cover and let rise for 3 hours.
4. Preheat oven to 375°F (190°C). Shape dough into a round loaf and place on a baking sheet.
5. Bake for 35 minutes or until the crust is firm.
6. Cool before slicing.

Nutritional Values (per slice):

- Calories: 130
- Carbohydrates: 26g
- Protein: 4g
- Fat: 1g
- Fiber: 2g

Tips & Tricks:

- **Flavor Boost:** Add caraway seeds for a traditional pumpernickel flavor.
- **Storage Tip:** Wrap in a cloth and store at room temperature for up to 3 days.

Rustic Potato Loaf

- **Preparation Time:** 30 minutes (plus 2 hours rising time)
- **Cooking Time:** 40 minutes
- **Servings:** 1 loaf (approx. 12 slices)

Ingredients:

- 1 cup sourdough discard
- 3 cups all-purpose flour
- 1 ½ cups mashed potatoes (no added butter or milk)
- ¾ cup warm water
- 1 ½ tsp salt

Directions:

1. In a large bowl, mix sourdough discard, mashed potatoes, and warm water until well combined.
2. Add flour and salt, kneading until a smooth dough forms. Cover and let rise for 2 hours.
3. Preheat oven to 400°F (200°C). Shape into a round loaf and place on a baking sheet.
4. Bake for 35-40 minutes, or until the crust is golden and the loaf sounds hollow when tapped.
5. Allow to cool on a wire rack before slicing.

Nutritional Values (per slice):

- Calories: 140
- Carbohydrates: 26g
- Protein: 4g
- Fat: 0.5g
- Fiber: 1g

Tips & Tricks:

- **Texture Tip:** For a softer texture, increase the amount of mashed potatoes.
- **Storage:** Wrap in foil and store at room temperature for up to 3 days.

Honey Whole Wheat Bread

- **Preparation Time:** 20 minutes (plus 1 ½ hours rising time)
- **Cooking Time:** 30 minutes
- **Servings:** 1 loaf (approx. 12 slices)

Ingredients:

- 1 cup sourdough discard
- 2 cups whole wheat flour
- 1 ½ cups all-purpose flour
- 1 ½ cups warm water
- 3 tbsp honey
- 1 ½ tsp salt

Directions:

1. In a large bowl, combine sourdough discard, warm water, and honey.
2. Gradually add the flours and salt, kneading until the dough is smooth.
3. Cover and let rise for 1 ½ hours in a warm place.
4. Preheat oven to 375°F (190°C). Shape the dough into a loaf and place in a greased loaf pan.
5. Bake for 30-35 minutes, or until the top is golden and the loaf sounds hollow when tapped.

6. Let cool before slicing.

Nutritional Values (per slice):
- Calories: 160
- Carbohydrates: 30g
- Protein: 5g
- Fat: 1g
- Fiber: 3g

Tips & Tricks:
- **Flavor Tip:** For added flavor, sprinkle oats on top before baking.
- **Serving Suggestion:** This bread pairs well with honey butter.

Garlic Knots

- **Preparation Time:** 15 minutes (plus 1 hour rising time)
- **Cooking Time:** 20 minutes
- **Servings:** 12 garlic knots

Ingredients:
- 1 cup sourdough discard
- 3 cups all-purpose flour
- ¾ cup warm water
- 2 tbsp olive oil
- 1 tsp salt
- 3 cloves garlic, minced
- 1 tbsp chopped parsley

Directions:
1. In a large bowl, mix sourdough discard, warm water, and olive oil.
2. Gradually add flour and salt, kneading until smooth. Cover and let rise for 1 hour.
3. Preheat oven to 375°F (190°C). Divide dough into 12 pieces, roll into strips, and tie into knots.
4. Place knots on a baking sheet and bake for 15-20 minutes, until golden.
5. While baking, heat olive oil in a small pan with minced garlic and parsley. Brush the garlic mixture over the knots once they are out of the oven.

Nutritional Values (per knot):
- Calories: 90
- Carbohydrates: 15g
- Protein: 2g
- Fat: 3g
- Fiber: 1g

Tips & Tricks:
- **Serving Tip:** Serve warm with marinara sauce for dipping.
- **Storage:** Store in an airtight container at room temperature for up to 2 days.

Sourdough Pretzel Bites

- **Preparation Time:** 20 minutes (plus 1 hour rising time)
- **Cooking Time:** 15 minutes
- **Servings:** 20 pretzel bites

Ingredients:
- 1 cup sourdough discard
- 2 cups all-purpose flour

- ½ cup warm water
- 1 tbsp sugar
- 1 tsp salt
- 4 cups water (for boiling)
- ¼ cup baking soda
- Coarse salt for sprinkling

Directions:

1. In a bowl, mix sourdough discard, warm water, sugar, and salt until smooth.
2. Gradually add flour, kneading until a soft dough forms. Cover and let rise for 1 hour.
3. Preheat oven to 425°F (220°C). Divide dough into small pieces and roll each piece into a ball.
4. Boil 4 cups of water with baking soda in a large pot. Drop pretzel bites into the boiling water for 20-30 seconds, then remove and place on a baking sheet.
5. Sprinkle with coarse salt and bake for 12-15 minutes or until golden brown.

Nutritional Values (per bite):

- Calories: 40
- Carbohydrates: 8g
- Protein: 1g
- Fat: 0g
- Fiber: 0.5g

Tips & Tricks:

- **For a soft texture,** avoid over-baking.
- **Serving Suggestion:** Serve with mustard or cheese dip for a classic pretzel experience.

Cheddar Biscuits

- **Preparation Time:** 15 minutes
- **Cooking Time:** 12-15 minutes
- **Servings:** 12 biscuits

Ingredients:

- 1 cup sourdough discard
- 2 cups all-purpose flour
- ½ cup cold butter, cubed
- 1 cup shredded cheddar cheese
- ¾ cup milk
- 1 tbsp baking powder
- 1 tsp salt

Directions:

1. Preheat oven to 425°F (220°C). In a bowl, combine flour, baking powder, and salt.
2. Cut in the cold butter until the mixture resembles coarse crumbs. Stir in the cheese.
3. Add sourdough discard and milk, mixing until just combined.
4. Drop spoonfuls of dough onto a greased baking sheet and bake for 12-15 minutes, until golden brown.

Nutritional Values (per biscuit):

- Calories: 150
- Carbohydrates: 20g
- Protein: 5g

- Fat: 6g
- Fiber: 1g

Tips & Tricks:
- **For extra flavor,** add a pinch of garlic powder to the dough.
- **Storage Tip:** Store in an airtight container at room temperature for up to 2 days.

Buttery Brioche Rolls

- **Preparation Time:** 30 minutes (plus 3 hours rising time)
- **Cooking Time:** 20 minutes
- **Servings:** 12 rolls

Ingredients:
- 1 cup sourdough discard
- 3 cups all-purpose flour
- ½ cup butter, softened
- ¼ cup sugar
- 3 large eggs
- ½ cup warm milk
- 1 tsp salt

Directions:
1. In a bowl, mix sourdough discard, warm milk, and sugar until smooth.
2. Add flour, eggs, softened butter, and salt, kneading until smooth. Cover and let rise for 2 hours.
3. Punch down the dough, divide into 12 rolls, and place on a greased baking sheet. Cover and let rise for 1 more hour.
4. Preheat oven to 375°F (190°C). Brush the tops with milk and bake for 20 minutes, or until golden brown.

Nutritional Values (per roll):
- Calories: 210
- Carbohydrates: 25g
- Protein: 5g
- Fat: 9g
- Fiber: 1g

Tips & Tricks:
- **Flavor Tip:** Add a dash of vanilla extract for a sweet hint.
- **Make Ahead:** These rolls freeze well for up to 2 months.

Herb Cracker Breads

- **Preparation Time:** 20 minutes
- **Cooking Time:** 15 minutes
- **Servings:** 20 crackers

Ingredients:
- 1 cup sourdough discard
- 1 ½ cups all-purpose flour
- ¼ cup olive oil
- 1 tbsp mixed dried herbs (e.g., rosemary, thyme, basil)
- ½ tsp salt

Directions:
1. Preheat oven to 350°F (175°C). In a bowl, combine sourdough discard, flour, olive oil, salt, and herbs.
2. Knead lightly and roll the dough out on a floured surface until thin.

3. Cut into squares and place on a baking sheet lined with parchment paper. Prick each cracker with a fork.

4. Bake for 12-15 minutes, or until golden and crispy.

Nutritional Values (per cracker):

- Calories: 30
- Carbohydrates: 5g
- Protein: 1g
- Fat: 1g
- Fiber: 0.2g

Tips & Tricks:

- **For extra crunch,** bake for an additional 2-3 minutes.
- **Serving Suggestion:** Pair with cheese or hummus for a delicious snack.

Apple Cinnamon Quick Bread

- **Preparation Time:** 15 minutes
- **Cooking Time:** 45 minutes
- **Servings:** 1 loaf (approx. 10 slices)

Ingredients:

- 1 cup sourdough discard
- 2 cups all-purpose flour
- 1 cup grated apple
- ¾ cup sugar
- ½ cup milk
- ¼ cup melted butter
- 1 tbsp ground cinnamon
- 1 tsp baking powder
- ½ tsp salt

Directions:

1. Preheat oven to 350°F (175°C). In a large bowl, combine flour, sugar, baking powder, cinnamon, and salt.
2. In another bowl, mix sourdough discard, milk, and melted butter.
3. Add the dry ingredients to the wet ingredients, followed by the grated apple, and stir until just combined.
4. Pour into a greased loaf pan and bake for 45-50 minutes, or until a toothpick comes out clean.

Nutritional Values (per slice):

- Calories: 160
- Carbohydrates: 30g
- Protein: 3g
- Fat: 4g
- Fiber: 1g

Tips & Tricks:

- **Flavor Variation:** Add a handful of chopped walnuts for added texture.
- **Serving Suggestion:** Delicious when served warm with a spread of butter.

Rye Bread

- **Preparation Time:** 25 minutes (plus 2 hours rising time)
- **Cooking Time:** 35 minutes
- **Servings:** 1 loaf (approx. 10 slices)

Ingredients:

- 1 cup sourdough discard
- 1 ½ cups rye flour
- 1 ½ cups all-purpose flour
- 1 ¼ cups warm water
- 1 tbsp molasses
- 1 tsp salt
- 1 tbsp caraway seeds (optional)

Directions:

1. In a large bowl, mix sourdough discard, warm water, and molasses.
2. Add rye flour, all-purpose flour, salt, and caraway seeds (if using). Knead until a smooth dough forms.
3. Cover and let rise for 2 hours or until doubled in size.
4. Preheat oven to 400°F (200°C). Shape dough into a round loaf and place on a baking sheet.
5. Bake for 30-35 minutes, or until the crust is firm and the loaf sounds hollow when tapped.
6. Let cool before slicing.

Nutritional Values (per slice):

- Calories: 130
- Carbohydrates: 24g
- Protein: 4g
- Fat: 1g
- Fiber: 2g

Tips & Tricks:

- **Flavor Tip:** For a stronger rye flavor, increase the caraway seeds.
- **Storage:** Wrap in a cloth and store at room temperature for up to 3 days.

Cranberry Almond Loaf

- **Preparation Time:** 15 minutes (plus 1 ½ hours rising time)
- **Cooking Time:** 45 minutes
- **Servings:** 1 loaf (approx. 12 slices)

Ingredients:

- 1 cup sourdough discard
- 3 cups all-purpose flour
- 1 cup warm water
- ½ cup dried cranberries
- ½ cup sliced almonds
- ¼ cup honey
- 1 tsp salt

Directions:

1. In a bowl, mix sourdough discard, warm water, and honey until well combined.
2. Add flour, salt, cranberries, and almonds, kneading until a soft dough forms.
3. Cover and let rise for 1 ½ hours in a warm place.
4. Preheat oven to 375°F (190°C). Shape the dough into a loaf and place in a greased loaf pan.
5. Bake for 40-45 minutes, or until golden brown and the loaf sounds hollow when tapped.
6. Let cool before slicing.

Nutritional Values (per slice):

- Calories: 160
- Carbohydrates: 28g
- Protein: 4g
- Fat: 3g
- Fiber: 1g

Tips & Tricks:

- **Serving Suggestion:** This loaf pairs well with cream cheese or a drizzle of honey.
- **Storage Tip:** Wrap tightly in plastic wrap and store at room temperature for up to 3 days.

Chocolate Babka

- **Preparation Time:** 30 minutes (plus 2 hours rising time)
- **Cooking Time:** 35 minutes
- **Servings:** 1 loaf (approx. 12 slices)

Ingredients:

- 1 cup sourdough discard
- 3 cups all-purpose flour
- ½ cup warm milk
- ½ cup sugar
- ¼ cup butter, softened
- 2 large eggs
- ½ tsp salt
- **Filling:**
    - 1 cup chocolate chips
    - ¼ cup butter, melted
    - 2 tbsp cocoa powder
    - ¼ cup sugar

Directions:

1. In a bowl, combine sourdough discard, warm milk, sugar, eggs, and salt.
2. Gradually add flour and softened butter, kneading until smooth. Cover and let rise for 1 ½ - 2 hours.
3. Roll the dough into a rectangle. Spread melted butter, sprinkle cocoa powder, sugar, and chocolate chips.
4. Roll the dough, cut lengthwise, and twist. Place in a greased loaf pan.
5. Preheat oven to 350°F (175°C) and bake for 30-35 minutes until golden.
6. Let cool before slicing.

Nutritional Values (per slice):

- Calories: 220
- Carbohydrates: 30g
- Protein: 5g
- Fat: 9g
- Fiber: 1g

Tips & Tricks:

- **For extra decadence,** drizzle with melted chocolate once cooled.
- **Storage Tip:** Wrap in foil and store at room temperature for up to 2 days.

Rustic Country Bread

- **Preparation Time:** 20 minutes (plus 4 hours rising time)
- **Cooking Time:** 40 minutes
- **Servings:** 1 loaf (approx. 12 slices)

Ingredients:

- 1 cup sourdough discard
- 4 cups all-purpose flour
- 1 ½ cups warm water
- 1 ½ tsp salt

Directions:

1. In a bowl, mix sourdough discard and warm water. Gradually add flour and salt, kneading until smooth.
2. Cover and let rise in a warm spot for 4 hours or until doubled in size.
3. Preheat oven to 450°F (230°C). Shape dough into a round loaf and place on a baking sheet.
4. Bake for 35-40 minutes, or until crusty and golden brown.
5. Allow to cool on a wire rack before slicing.

Nutritional Values (per slice):

- Calories: 120
- Carbohydrates: 23g
- Protein: 4g
- Fat: 0.5g
- Fiber: 1g

Tips & Tricks:

- **Crust Tip:** Place a small dish of water in the oven to create steam for a crustier texture.
- **Serving Suggestion:** Serve with olive oil and balsamic vinegar for dipping.

Potato Focaccia

- **Preparation Time:** 20 minutes (plus 2 hours rising time)
- **Cooking Time:** 25 minutes
- **Servings:** 1 focaccia (approx. 12 squares)

Ingredients:

- 1 cup sourdough discard
- 3 cups all-purpose flour
- 1 cup mashed potatoes
- 1 cup warm water
- 2 tbsp olive oil, plus extra for drizzling
- 1 tsp salt
- Fresh rosemary (for topping)

Directions:

1. In a bowl, combine sourdough discard, mashed potatoes, warm water, and olive oil.
2. Add flour and salt, kneading until a smooth dough forms. Cover and let rise for 2 hours.
3. Preheat oven to 400°F (200°C). Spread dough on a greased baking sheet, pressing in fresh rosemary.
4. Drizzle with olive oil and bake for 20-25 minutes, or until golden brown.
5. Let cool slightly before cutting into squares.

Nutritional Values (per square):

- Calories: 130
- Carbohydrates: 22g
- Protein: 3g

- Fat: 3g
- Fiber: 1g

Tips & Tricks:
- **Serving Suggestion:** Serve with marinara sauce for dipping.
- **Texture Tip:** Add more olive oil for a softer, richer focaccia.

Cinnamon Raisin Swirl Bread

- **Preparation Time:** 25 minutes (plus 2 hours rising time)
- **Cooking Time:** 35 minutes
- **Servings:** 1 loaf (approx. 12 slices)

Ingredients:
- 1 cup sourdough discard
- 3 cups all-purpose flour
- 1 cup warm milk
- ¼ cup sugar
- 1 tsp salt
- 1 tbsp cinnamon
- ½ cup raisins
- **Filling:**
    - 2 tbsp melted butter
    - ¼ cup sugar
    - 1 tbsp cinnamon

Directions:
1. In a large bowl, combine sourdough discard, warm milk, sugar, and salt. Gradually add flour, kneading until smooth.
2. Cover and let rise for 1 ½ to 2 hours.
3. Roll the dough into a rectangle. Brush with melted butter and sprinkle with cinnamon and sugar mixture. Add raisins.
4. Roll up the dough tightly and place in a greased loaf pan.
5. Preheat oven to 350°F (175°C) and bake for 30-35 minutes until golden.
6. Allow to cool before slicing.

Nutritional Values (per slice):
- Calories: 160
- Carbohydrates: 30g
- Protein: 4g
- Fat: 2g
- Fiber: 1g

Tips & Tricks:
- **For extra sweetness,** add a powdered sugar glaze on top once cooled.
- **Storage Tip:** Wrap in plastic wrap and store at room temperature for up to 3 days.

Quinoa Bread

- **Preparation Time:** 20 minutes (plus 1 ½ hours rising time)
- **Cooking Time:** 35 minutes
- **Servings:** 1 loaf (approx. 10 slices)

Ingredients:
- 1 cup sourdough discard
- 3 cups all-purpose flour
- ½ cup cooked quinoa

- 1 cup warm water
- 2 tbsp honey
- 1 tsp salt

Directions:

1. In a mixing bowl, combine sourdough discard, warm water, and honey.
2. Add flour, salt, and cooked quinoa. Knead until a smooth dough forms.
3. Cover and let rise in a warm place for 1 ½ hours.
4. Preheat oven to 375°F (190°C). Shape the dough into a loaf and place in a greased loaf pan.
5. Bake for 35-40 minutes until golden brown.
6. Let cool before slicing.

Nutritional Values (per slice):

- Calories: 150
- Carbohydrates: 28g
- Protein: 4g
- Fat: 1g
- Fiber: 1g

Tips & Tricks:

- **For a nuttier flavor,** add a handful of toasted sesame seeds.
- **Storage Tip:** Wrap in foil and store at room temperature for up to 3 days.

Garlic Parmesan Breadsticks

- **Preparation Time:** 15 minutes (plus 1 hour rising time)
- **Cooking Time:** 15 minutes
- **Servings:** 12 breadsticks

Ingredients:

- 1 cup sourdough discard
- 2 cups all-purpose flour
- ½ cup warm water
- 2 tbsp olive oil
- 1 tsp salt
- ½ cup grated Parmesan cheese
- 2 cloves garlic, minced

Directions:

1. In a bowl, mix sourdough discard, warm water, and olive oil.
2. Add flour and salt, kneading until smooth. Cover and let rise for 1 hour.
3. Preheat oven to 400°F (200°C). Divide dough into 12 pieces, roll into sticks, and place on a baking sheet.
4. Mix minced garlic with Parmesan cheese, and sprinkle over the breadsticks.
5. Bake for 12-15 minutes or until golden brown.

Nutritional Values (per breadstick):

- Calories: 90
- Carbohydrates: 15g
- Protein: 3g
- Fat: 2g
- Fiber: 0.5g

Tips & Tricks:

- **Serving Suggestion:** Serve warm with marinara or garlic butter for dipping.

- **Make Ahead:** These breadsticks freeze well and can be reheated in the oven.

Soft Hamburger Buns

- **Preparation Time:** 30 minutes (plus 2 hours rising time)
- **Cooking Time:** 20 minutes
- **Servings:** 8 buns

Ingredients:

- 1 cup sourdough discard
- 3 cups all-purpose flour
- ½ cup warm milk
- ¼ cup melted butter
- 1 tbsp sugar
- 1 tsp salt
- 1 large egg

Directions:

1. In a mixing bowl, combine sourdough discard, warm milk, melted butter, sugar, and salt.
2. Gradually add flour, kneading until a smooth dough forms. Cover and let rise for 1 ½ - 2 hours.
3. Preheat oven to 375°F (190°C). Divide the dough into 8 equal portions, shape into buns, and place on a baking sheet.
4. Brush the tops with beaten egg for a glossy finish, then bake for 18-20 minutes until golden.
5. Cool on a wire rack before slicing.

Nutritional Values (per bun):

- Calories: 160
- Carbohydrates: 25g
- Protein: 4g
- Fat: 4g
- Fiber: 1g

Tips & Tricks:

- **For extra softness,** cover the buns with a cloth as they cool.
- **Serving Suggestion:** Perfect for burgers, sandwiches, or sliders.

Pumpkin Quick Bread

- **Preparation Time:** 15 minutes
- **Cooking Time:** 50 minutes
- **Servings:** 1 loaf (approx. 10 slices)

Ingredients:

- 1 cup sourdough discard
- 2 cups all-purpose flour
- 1 cup canned pumpkin puree
- ¾ cup sugar
- ½ cup milk
- ¼ cup vegetable oil
- 1 tsp baking powder
- 1 tsp cinnamon
- ½ tsp salt

Directions:

1. Preheat oven to 350°F (175°C). In a large bowl, combine flour, baking powder, cinnamon, and salt.

2. In another bowl, mix sourdough discard, pumpkin puree, sugar, milk, and oil until well combined.
3. Add the dry ingredients to the wet ingredients, stirring until just combined.
4. Pour into a greased loaf pan and bake for 50-55 minutes, or until a toothpick inserted comes out clean.
5. Allow to cool before slicing.

Nutritional Values (per slice):
- Calories: 150
- Carbohydrates: 28g
- Protein: 3g
- Fat: 3g
- Fiber: 1g

Tips & Tricks:
- **Flavor Variation:** Add a pinch of nutmeg or cloves for extra warmth.
- **Serving Suggestion:** Delicious with a spread of cream cheese or honey butter.

Spinach and Herb Rolls

- **Preparation Time:** 20 minutes (plus 1 ½ hours rising time)
- **Cooking Time:** 25 minutes
- **Servings:** 12 rolls

Ingredients:
- 1 cup sourdough discard
- 3 cups all-purpose flour
- 1 cup warm water
- 1 tbsp olive oil
- 1 tsp salt
- 1 cup fresh spinach, chopped
- 1 tbsp mixed fresh herbs (such as rosemary, thyme, and basil)

Directions:
1. In a large bowl, mix sourdough discard, warm water, and olive oil.
2. Gradually add flour, salt, spinach, and herbs, kneading until a smooth dough forms.
3. Cover and let rise for 1 ½ hours in a warm place.
4. Preheat oven to 375°F (190°C). Divide the dough into 12 equal pieces and shape into rolls.
5. Place rolls on a baking sheet and bake for 20-25 minutes until golden.
6. Let cool slightly before serving.

Nutritional Values (per roll):
- Calories: 120
- Carbohydrates: 20g
- Protein: 3g
- Fat: 2g
- Fiber: 1g

Tips & Tricks:
- **Serving Suggestion:** These rolls pair well with soups and salads.
- **Storage Tip:** Store in an airtight container at room temperature for up to 2 days.

Oatmeal Bread

- **Preparation Time:** 20 minutes (plus 2 hours rising time)
- **Cooking Time:** 35 minutes
- **Servings:** 1 loaf (approx. 10 slices)

Ingredients:

- 1 cup sourdough discard
- 3 cups all-purpose flour
- ½ cup rolled oats, plus extra for topping
- 1 cup warm water
- 2 tbsp honey
- 1 tsp salt

Directions:

1. In a large bowl, combine sourdough discard, warm water, honey, and salt.
2. Gradually add flour and oats, kneading until smooth.
3. Cover and let rise for 2 hours or until doubled in size.
4. Preheat oven to 375°F (190°C). Shape the dough into a loaf and place in a greased loaf pan. Sprinkle extra oats on top.
5. Bake for 35-40 minutes or until golden brown.
6. Let cool before slicing.

Nutritional Values (per slice):

- Calories: 130
- Carbohydrates: 25g
- Protein: 4g
- Fat: 1g
- Fiber: 1g

Tips & Tricks:

- **Flavor Tip:** Add a handful of sunflower or flax seeds for added texture.
- **Serving Suggestion:** Delicious toasted with butter or jam.

Olive and Sun-Dried Tomato Bread

- **Preparation Time:** 25 minutes (plus 2 hours rising time)
- **Cooking Time:** 35 minutes
- **Servings:** 1 loaf (approx. 10 slices)

Ingredients:

- 1 cup sourdough discard
- 3 cups all-purpose flour
- 1 cup warm water
- 1 tbsp olive oil
- 1 tsp salt
- ½ cup chopped black olives
- ¼ cup chopped sun-dried tomatoes

Directions:

1. In a mixing bowl, combine sourdough discard, warm water, and olive oil.
2. Add flour, salt, olives, and sun-dried tomatoes, kneading until a smooth dough forms.
3. Cover and let rise for 2 hours in a warm place.

4. Preheat oven to 400°F (200°C). Shape the dough into a round loaf and place on a baking sheet.
5. Bake for 30-35 minutes, or until golden brown.
6. Let cool slightly before slicing.

Nutritional Values (per slice):

- Calories: 140
- Carbohydrates: 24g
- Protein: 4g
- Fat: 3g
- Fiber: 1g

Tips & Tricks:

- **Flavor Variation:** Add fresh rosemary for an herby twist.
- **Serving Suggestion:** This bread pairs well with a cheese platter or as a base for bruschetta.

CHAPTER 3: IRRESISTIBLE BITES & SAVORY TREATS

Crispy Parmesan Cheese Straws

Preparation Time: 15 minutes
Cooking Time: 20 minutes
Servings: 20 straws

Ingredients:

- 1 cup sourdough discard
- 1 cup all-purpose flour
- 1/2 cup unsalted butter, chilled and cubed
- 1/2 teaspoon salt
- 1/2 teaspoon black pepper
- 1 cup grated Parmesan cheese
- 1 teaspoon dried thyme (optional)
- 1 teaspoon garlic powder

Directions:

1. Preheat the oven to 375°F (190°C) and line a baking sheet with parchment paper.
2. In a mixing bowl, combine the flour, salt, pepper, and garlic powder. Add the chilled butter and cut it into the flour until the mixture resembles coarse crumbs.
3. Stir in the sourdough discard until the dough begins to come together.
4. Gently fold in the Parmesan cheese and thyme.
5. Roll the dough out on a lightly floured surface to about 1/4-inch thickness. Cut into 1/2-inch-wide strips.
6. Place the strips onto the prepared baking sheet and twist each strip to create a spiral shape.
7. Bake for 15–20 minutes or until golden brown and crisp.
8. Allow to cool slightly before serving.

Nutritional Values (per straw):

- Calories: 90
- Fat: 6g
- Carbohydrates: 8g
- Protein: 3g

Tips & Tricks:

- **For extra flavor**, sprinkle a pinch of paprika or chili powder for a slight kick.
- **Storage**: These cheese straws keep well in an airtight container for up to 5 days.

Herbed Garlic Breadsticks

Preparation Time: 20 minutes
Cooking Time: 15 minutes
Servings: 10 breadsticks

Ingredients:

- 1 cup sourdough discard
- 1 cup all-purpose flour
- 1/2 teaspoon salt
- 1 teaspoon garlic powder
- 1/2 teaspoon dried oregano
- 1/2 teaspoon dried basil
- 2 tablespoons olive oil, plus more for brushing
- Sea salt and black pepper to taste

Directions:

1. Preheat the oven to 400°F (200°C) and line a baking sheet with parchment paper.
2. In a large bowl, combine the flour, salt, garlic powder, oregano, and basil.
3. Add the sourdough discard and olive oil, stirring until a soft dough forms. Knead the dough lightly on a floured surface.
4. Divide the dough into 10 equal portions and roll each into a long breadstick shape.
5. Place the breadsticks on the prepared baking sheet and brush with a light coat of olive oil. Sprinkle sea salt and pepper over each breadstick.
6. Bake for 12–15 minutes or until golden and crisp on the outside.
7. Serve warm with a side of marinara or garlic butter.

Nutritional Values (per breadstick):

- Calories: 100
- Fat: 4g
- Carbohydrates: 14g
- Protein: 2g

Tips & Tricks:

- **Variations**: Try adding grated Parmesan or a sprinkle of red pepper flakes for a little heat.
- **Serving suggestion**: Pair with dips like hummus or tzatziki for a Mediterranean twist.

Soft Pretzel Bites

Preparation Time: 25 minutes
Cooking Time: 15 minutes
Servings: 30 bites

Ingredients:

- 1 cup sourdough discard
- 1 1/2 cups all-purpose flour
- 1/2 teaspoon salt
- 1 tablespoon sugar
- 1/2 teaspoon baking powder
- 3 cups water
- 1/4 cup baking soda
- Coarse salt, for sprinkling
- 2 tablespoons melted butter

Directions:

1. Preheat the oven to 425°F (220°C) and line a baking sheet with parchment paper.
2. In a bowl, combine the flour, salt, sugar, and baking powder. Stir in the sourdough discard until a dough forms.
3. Knead the dough for about 5 minutes until smooth and elastic.
4. Divide the dough into small pieces (about 1-inch each) to form bite-sized balls.
5. In a saucepan, bring water to a boil and add the baking soda. Drop the dough balls into the boiling water for 30 seconds, then remove with a slotted spoon.

6. Place the boiled bites on the prepared baking sheet, brush with melted butter, and sprinkle with coarse salt.
7. Bake for 12–15 minutes or until golden brown.
8. Serve warm with mustard or cheese dip.

Nutritional Values (per bite):

- Calories: 45
- Fat: 1g
- Carbohydrates: 8g
- Protein: 1g

Tips & Tricks:

- **Flavor option**: Brush with melted garlic butter instead of plain butter for a garlic-flavored twist.
- **Serving idea**: Great for parties or movie nights—pair with a warm cheese sauce for dipping.

Mozzarella Stuffed Rolls

Preparation Time: 20 minutes
Cooking Time: 25 minutes
Servings: 12 rolls

Ingredients:

- 1 cup sourdough discard
- 1 1/2 cups all-purpose flour
- 1/2 teaspoon salt
- 1 teaspoon sugar
- 1 tablespoon olive oil
- 12 mozzarella cheese sticks or cubes
- 1 tablespoon melted butter
- Fresh parsley, chopped (for garnish)

Directions:

1. Preheat the oven to 375°F (190°C) and line a baking sheet with parchment paper.
2. In a bowl, mix flour, salt, and sugar. Add sourdough discard and olive oil to form a soft dough.
3. Knead the dough for about 5 minutes, then divide into 12 equal portions.
4. Flatten each piece of dough and wrap around a mozzarella stick or cube, pinching the edges to seal.
5. Place each roll on the baking sheet, brush with melted butter, and sprinkle with parsley.
6. Bake for 20–25 minutes or until the rolls are golden brown.
7. Serve warm, with marinara sauce for dipping.

Nutritional Values (per roll):

- Calories: 120
- Fat: 5g
- Carbohydrates: 14g
- Protein: 5g

Tips & Tricks:

- **Add herbs**: Add Italian seasoning to the dough for extra flavor.
- **Serving tip**: These rolls make a great appetizer or snack for kids.

Kale and Herb Chips

Preparation Time: 10 minutes
Cooking Time: 10 minutes
Servings: 4

Ingredients:

- 1 cup sourdough discard
- 2 cups fresh kale leaves, stems removed
- 1 tablespoon olive oil
- 1/2 teaspoon salt
- 1/2 teaspoon garlic powder
- 1/2 teaspoon smoked paprika
- Freshly ground black pepper, to taste

Directions:

1. Preheat the oven to 350°F (175°C) and line a baking sheet with parchment paper.
2. Rinse and thoroughly dry the kale leaves.
3. In a large bowl, toss the kale with olive oil until evenly coated.
4. Add sourdough discard, salt, garlic powder, smoked paprika, and black pepper. Toss until the kale leaves are fully coated.
5. Arrange the kale leaves in a single layer on the prepared baking sheet.
6. Bake for 8–10 minutes or until the edges are crisp and the kale has shrunk slightly. Watch closely to prevent burning.
7. Allow to cool slightly and serve immediately.

Nutritional Values (per serving):

- Calories: 70
- Fat: 4g
- Carbohydrates: 6g
- Protein: 2g

Tips & Tricks:

- **Make it spicy**: Add a pinch of cayenne pepper for an extra kick.
- **Storage**: Keep leftover chips in an airtight container, but note that they may lose crispiness after a day.

Sourdough Dumplings

Preparation Time: 20 minutes
Cooking Time: 25 minutes
Servings: 4

Ingredients:

- 1 cup sourdough discard
- 1 cup all-purpose flour
- 1/2 teaspoon salt
- 1/2 teaspoon baking powder
- 1/4 cup cold water
- 1 tablespoon fresh parsley, chopped
- Broth of choice (vegetable, chicken, or beef) for cooking

Directions:

1. In a mixing bowl, combine flour, salt, and baking powder. Stir in the sourdough discard, water, and parsley until a soft dough forms.
2. Roll the dough into small dumplings (about 1 inch each).

3. Bring the broth to a simmer in a large pot. Drop the dumplings into the simmering broth.
4. Cover and cook for 20–25 minutes, or until the dumplings are tender and puffed up.
5. Serve warm, in the broth, as a hearty side or light main dish.

Nutritional Values (per serving):

- Calories: 120
- Fat: 1g
- Carbohydrates: 24g
- Protein: 3g

Tips & Tricks:

- **Add herbs**: Customize by adding fresh thyme or chives to the dumpling dough.
- **For extra richness**: Use bone broth or a well-seasoned stock for added flavor.

Savory Popovers with Cheddar

Preparation Time: 15 minutes
Cooking Time: 30 minutes
Servings: 12 popovers

Ingredients:

- 1 cup sourdough discard
- 1 cup all-purpose flour
- 1/2 teaspoon salt
- 3 large eggs
- 1 cup whole milk
- 1 cup grated cheddar cheese
- 1 tablespoon melted butter, for greasing

Directions:

1. Preheat the oven to 400°F (200°C) and grease a muffin tin with melted butter.
2. In a bowl, whisk together the sourdough discard, flour, salt, eggs, and milk until smooth.
3. Fold in the grated cheddar cheese.
4. Pour the batter into the prepared muffin tin, filling each cup about halfway.
5. Bake for 25–30 minutes, or until the popovers are puffed and golden brown.
6. Serve warm for best results.

Nutritional Values (per popover):

- Calories: 130
- Fat: 7g
- Carbohydrates: 11g
- Protein: 5g

Tips & Tricks:

- **Enhance flavor**: Add a pinch of garlic powder or fresh herbs like rosemary.
- **Serve immediately**: Popovers are best enjoyed fresh out of the oven.

Crab Cakes with Sourdough

Preparation Time: 25 minutes
Cooking Time: 10 minutes
Servings: 6 cakes

Ingredients:

- 1/2 cup sourdough discard
- 1 pound fresh lump crab meat, picked over for shells
- 1/2 cup breadcrumbs
- 1/4 cup mayonnaise
- 1 large egg, beaten
- 1 tablespoon Dijon mustard
- 1 tablespoon lemon juice
- 1/4 cup green onions, finely chopped
- Salt and pepper to taste
- 2 tablespoons olive oil, for frying

Directions:

1. In a large bowl, mix the sourdough discard, crab meat, breadcrumbs, mayonnaise, egg, Dijon mustard, lemon juice, and green onions. Season with salt and pepper.
2. Form the mixture into 6 equal-sized cakes.
3. Heat olive oil in a skillet over medium heat. Add the crab cakes and cook for 4–5 minutes per side, until golden brown.
4. Serve warm with lemon wedges or a side of tartar sauce.

Nutritional Values (per crab cake):

- Calories: 180
- Fat: 10g
- Carbohydrates: 8g
- Protein: 15g

Tips & Tricks:

- **Add a kick**: Mix in a pinch of cayenne pepper for added spice.
- **Chill the mixture**: Refrigerate the formed cakes for 15 minutes before frying to help them hold their shape.

Mediterranean Flatbreads

Preparation Time: 20 minutes
Cooking Time: 15 minutes
Servings: 4

Ingredients:

- 1 cup sourdough discard
- 1 cup all-purpose flour
- 1/2 teaspoon salt
- 1/2 teaspoon dried oregano
- 1/2 teaspoon dried thyme
- 2 tablespoons olive oil
- 1/2 cup crumbled feta cheese
- 1/4 cup chopped olives
- 1/4 cup diced tomatoes

Directions:

1. In a mixing bowl, combine the flour, salt, oregano, and thyme. Add the sourdough discard and olive oil, stirring until a soft dough forms.
2. Divide the dough into 4 equal portions and roll each into a thin round.
3. Place the rounds on a hot griddle or skillet, cooking each side for 3–4 minutes until lightly browned.
4. Top each flatbread with feta, olives, and tomatoes before serving.

Nutritional Values (per flatbread):

- Calories: 160
- Fat: 9g
- Carbohydrates: 14g
- Protein: 5g

Tips & Tricks:

- **Alternative toppings**: Try adding roasted red peppers or artichoke hearts.
- **Perfect with dips**: Serve with hummus or tzatziki for a complete Mediterranean snack.

Spinach and Feta Turnovers

Preparation Time: 25 minutes
Cooking Time: 20 minutes
Servings: 8 turnovers

Ingredients:

- 1 cup sourdough discard
- 1 cup all-purpose flour
- 1/2 teaspoon salt
- 2 tablespoons olive oil
- 1/2 cup cooked spinach, chopped
- 1/2 cup crumbled feta cheese
- 1 egg, beaten (for egg wash)

Directions:

1. Preheat the oven to 375°F (190°C) and line a baking sheet with parchment paper.
2. In a bowl, mix the flour, salt, sourdough discard, and olive oil to form a soft dough.
3. Divide the dough into 8 portions and roll each into a small round.
4. Fill each round with a spoonful of spinach and feta. Fold in half and pinch the edges to seal.
5. Brush each turnover with the beaten egg and place on the baking sheet.
6. Bake for 20 minutes or until golden brown. Serve warm.

Nutritional Values (per turnover):

- Calories: 120
- Fat: 6g
- Carbohydrates: 12g
- Protein: 4g

Tips & Tricks:

- **Use fresh herbs**: Add dill or parsley for added flavor.
- **Freezing option**: These turnovers freeze well—just reheat before serving.

Sourdough Empanadas

Preparation Time: 30 minutes
Cooking Time: 25 minutes
Servings: 10 empanadas

Ingredients:

- 1 cup sourdough discard
- 1 1/2 cups all-purpose flour
- 1/2 teaspoon salt
- 1/4 cup cold butter, cubed
- 1/4 cup cold water
- 1/2 pound ground beef or chicken

- 1/2 cup diced onions
- 1/4 cup diced bell pepper
- Salt and pepper to taste
- 1/2 teaspoon paprika
- 1 egg, beaten (for egg wash)

Directions:

1. Preheat oven to 375°F (190°C) and line a baking sheet with parchment paper.
2. In a mixing bowl, combine flour and salt. Add cold butter and mix until the dough forms coarse crumbs.
3. Stir in sourdough discard and cold water until a dough forms. Knead briefly, wrap in plastic, and chill for 15 minutes.
4. In a skillet, cook ground meat until browned. Add onions, bell pepper, salt, pepper, and paprika. Set aside.
5. Roll dough on a floured surface and cut into 4 inch circles.
6. Add a spoonful of filling to each circle, fold in half, and seal edges.
7. Brush with beaten egg and bake for 20–25 minutes until golden.

Nutritional Values (per empanada):

- Calories: 150
- Fat: 8g
- Carbohydrates: 13g
- Protein: 7g

Tips & Tricks:

- **Spice it up**: Add chili powder for extra heat.
- **Freezing option**: Freeze unbaked empanadas; bake when needed.

Flatbread with Olive Tapenade

Preparation Time: 20 minutes
Cooking Time: 10 minutes
Servings: 4 flatbreads

Ingredients:

- 1 cup sourdough discard
- 1 cup all-purpose flour
- 1/2 teaspoon salt
- 1 tablespoon olive oil
- 1/2 cup prepared olive tapenade
- 1 tablespoon fresh rosemary, chopped (optional)

Directions:

1. Combine flour, salt, sourdough discard, and olive oil to form a soft dough.
2. Divide dough into 4 portions, roll each portion into a thin circle.
3. Heat a skillet over medium heat, add a drizzle of olive oil, and cook each flatbread for 2–3 minutes per side until golden.
4. Spread olive tapenade on top of each flatbread, sprinkle with rosemary, and serve warm.

Nutritional Values (per flatbread):

- Calories: 110
- Fat: 4g
- Carbohydrates: 15g
- Protein: 2g

Tips & Tricks:
- **Add toppings**: Try adding crumbled feta or sun-dried tomatoes.
- **Perfect pairing**: Serve with a side salad for a light meal.

Cheesy Breadsticks

Preparation Time: 15 minutes
Cooking Time: 15 minutes
Servings: 8 breadsticks

Ingredients:
- 1 cup sourdough discard
- 1 cup all-purpose flour
- 1/2 teaspoon salt
- 1/2 teaspoon garlic powder
- 1/2 cup shredded mozzarella
- 1 tablespoon butter, melted
- 1 tablespoon chopped parsley, for garnish

Directions:
1. Preheat oven to 400°F (200°C) and line a baking sheet with parchment paper.
2. Mix flour, salt, garlic powder, and sourdough discard to form a dough.
3. Roll dough into an 8-inch square and sprinkle with mozzarella.
4. Cut into 8 strips and twist each one before placing on the baking sheet.
5. Brush with melted butter and bake for 12–15 minutes until golden.
6. Garnish with parsley and serve warm.

Nutritional Values (per breadstick):
- Calories: 90
- Fat: 3g
- Carbohydrates: 11g
- Protein: 3g

Tips & Tricks:
- **Spice it up**: Add red pepper flakes for a touch of heat.
- **Dipping suggestion**: Serve with marinara or garlic butter.

Stuffed Bread Rolls

Preparation Time: 30 minutes
Cooking Time: 20 minutes
Servings: 8 rolls

Ingredients:
- 1 cup sourdough discard
- 1 1/2 cups all-purpose flour
- 1/2 teaspoon salt
- 1 tablespoon sugar
- 1 tablespoon olive oil
- 8 slices of pepperoni or 1/4 cup cooked spinach
- 8 small cheese cubes
- 1 egg, beaten (for egg wash)

Directions:
1. Preheat oven to 375°F (190°C) and line a baking sheet with parchment paper.
2. In a bowl, mix flour, salt, sugar, sourdough discard, and olive oil to form a soft dough.

3. Divide dough into 8 portions and flatten each portion.

4. Place a slice of pepperoni and a cheese cube in each, then wrap the dough around to seal.

5. Place on the baking sheet, brush with egg wash, and bake for 20 minutes until golden.

Nutritional Values (per roll):

- Calories: 140
- Fat: 5g
- Carbohydrates: 18g
- Protein: 4g

Tips & Tricks:

- **Switch fillings**: Use cooked sausage or mushrooms for variety.
- **Serving idea**: These rolls are great as a lunchbox treat.

Grissini Sticks

Preparation Time: 20 minutes
Cooking Time: 12 minutes
Servings: 16 sticks

Ingredients:

- 1 cup sourdough discard
- 1 cup all-purpose flour
- 1/2 teaspoon salt
- 1 teaspoon dried rosemary
- 2 tablespoons olive oil
- Sea salt, for sprinkling

Directions:

1. Preheat oven to 375°F (190°C) and line a baking sheet with parchment paper.

2. Combine flour, salt, rosemary, sourdough discard, and olive oil to form a dough.

3. Roll dough into thin sticks and place on the baking sheet.

4. Sprinkle with sea salt and bake for 10–12 minutes until crisp.

5. Serve as an appetizer with dips.

Nutritional Values (per stick):

- Calories: 35
- Fat: 1g
- Carbohydrates: 5g
- Protein: 1g

Tips & Tricks:

- **Try different herbs**: Use thyme or oregano instead of rosemary.
- **Dipping ideas**: Serve with marinara or garlic aioli.

Sourdough Pizza Bites

Preparation Time: 15 minutes
Cooking Time: 15 minutes
Servings: 16 bites

Ingredients:

- 1 cup sourdough discard
- 1 cup all-purpose flour
- 1/2 teaspoon salt
- 1/4 teaspoon garlic powder
- 1/2 cup shredded mozzarella

- 1/4 cup mini pepperoni slices
- Marinara sauce, for dipping

Directions:

1. Preheat oven to 400°F (200°C) and line a baking sheet with parchment paper.
2. Mix flour, salt, garlic powder, and sourdough discard to form a dough.
3. Roll dough into small balls, flatten slightly, and press mozzarella and pepperoni on top.
4. Bake for 12–15 minutes until golden and cheese is melted.
5. Serve with marinara for dipping.

Nutritional Values (per bite):

- Calories: 60
- Fat: 2g
- Carbohydrates: 7g
- Protein: 2g

Tips & Tricks:

- **Make it veggie**: Use bell peppers or mushrooms instead of pepperoni.
- **Serving suggestion**: These are perfect for a kids' snack or party appetizer.

Roasted Red Pepper Crackers

Preparation Time: 15 minutes
Cooking Time: 12 minutes
Servings: 30 crackers

Ingredients:

- 1 cup sourdough discard
- 1 cup all-purpose flour
- 1/4 cup finely chopped roasted red peppers
- 1/2 teaspoon salt
- 1/2 teaspoon smoked paprika
- 1 tablespoon olive oil
- Sea salt, for sprinkling

Directions:

1. Preheat oven to 375°F (190°C) and line a baking sheet with parchment paper.
2. In a mixing bowl, combine flour, salt, smoked paprika, and sourdough discard.
3. Add roasted red peppers and olive oil, mixing until the dough forms.
4. Roll out the dough on a floured surface until thin, about 1/8 inch thick. Cut into squares or desired shapes.
5. Place crackers on the baking sheet and sprinkle with sea salt.
6. Bake for 10–12 minutes or until golden and crisp.
7. Allow to cool completely before serving.

Nutritional Values (per cracker):

- Calories: 20
- Fat: 0.5g
- Carbohydrates: 4g
- Protein: 0.5g

Tips & Tricks:

- **Extra crunch**: Brush with a bit of olive oil before baking for added crispiness.
- **Storage**: Keep in an airtight container for up to a week.

Stuffed Mini Peppers with Sourdough

Preparation Time: 15 minutes
Cooking Time: 10 minutes
Servings: 12 stuffed peppers

Ingredients:

- 1/2 cup sourdough discard
- 12 mini bell peppers, tops removed and seeds scooped out
- 1/2 cup cream cheese, softened
- 1/4 cup grated cheddar cheese
- 1/2 teaspoon garlic powder
- 1/2 teaspoon dried basil
- Salt and pepper, to taste

Directions:

1. Preheat the oven to 400°F (200°C) and line a baking sheet with parchment paper.
2. In a bowl, mix sourdough discard, cream cheese, cheddar, garlic powder, basil, salt, and pepper until smooth.
3. Stuff each mini pepper with the cheese mixture and place on the baking sheet.
4. Bake for 10 minutes or until peppers are slightly softened and cheese is bubbly.
5. Serve warm as a delightful appetizer or snack.

Nutritional Values (per stuffed pepper):

- Calories: 50
- Fat: 4g
- Carbohydrates: 2g
- Protein: 2g

Tips & Tricks:

- **Variation**: Add finely chopped cooked bacon for an extra layer of flavor.
- **Serving suggestion**: Garnish with chopped parsley or chives.

Herbed Cheese Straws

Preparation Time: 20 minutes
Cooking Time: 15 minutes
Servings: 20 straws

Ingredients:

- 1 cup sourdough discard
- 1 cup all-purpose flour
- 1/2 cup cold butter, cubed
- 1 cup shredded Parmesan cheese
- 1 teaspoon dried thyme
- 1/2 teaspoon garlic powder
- Salt and pepper, to taste

Directions:

1. Preheat oven to 375°F (190°C) and line a baking sheet with parchment paper.

2. In a food processor, combine flour, salt, pepper, garlic powder, and thyme.

3. Add butter and pulse until the mixture resembles coarse crumbs.

4. Add sourdough discard and Parmesan cheese, pulsing until dough comes together.

5. Roll out the dough on a floured surface to about 1/4 inch thick. Cut into 1/2-inch-wide strips and twist each strip into a spiral.

6. Place on the baking sheet and bake for 12–15 minutes until golden brown.

7. Cool slightly before serving.

Nutritional Values (per straw):

- Calories: 70
- Fat: 4g
- Carbohydrates: 6g
- Protein: 2g

Tips & Tricks:

- **Make it spicy**: Add a pinch of red pepper flakes for a touch of heat.
- **Storage**: These keep well in an airtight container for up to a week.

Samosas with Sourdough Pastry

Preparation Time: 30 minutes
Cooking Time: 25 minutes
Servings: 12 samosas

Ingredients:

- 1 cup sourdough discard
- 1 1/2 cups all-purpose flour
- 1/2 teaspoon salt
- 1/4 cup cold butter, cubed
- 1/4 cup cold water
- 1 cup boiled and diced potatoes
- 1/2 cup green peas
- 1/2 teaspoon cumin seeds
- 1/2 teaspoon garam masala
- Salt and pepper, to taste
- Vegetable oil for frying

Directions:

1. In a bowl, combine flour and salt. Cut in butter until the mixture resembles crumbs.

2. Stir in sourdough discard and cold water to form a dough. Wrap and chill for 15 minutes.

3. In a skillet, cook cumin seeds until fragrant. Add potatoes, peas, garam masala, salt, and pepper.

4. Divide the dough into 12 portions, roll each into a circle, and fill with the potato mixture.

5. Fold into a triangle and seal the edges with a fork.

6. Fry in hot oil for 3–4 minutes per side or bake at 375°F (190°C) for 20 minutes until golden brown.

Nutritional Values (per samosa):

- Calories: 120
- Fat: 4g
- Carbohydrates: 18g
- Protein: 2g

Tips & Tricks:

- **Baking option**: For a healthier version, bake instead of frying.
- **Add flavor**: For extra spice, add diced green chilies or a dash of turmeric.

CHAPTER 4: COMFORTING MAIN DISHES

Hearty Burrito Bowls

Preparation Time: 20 minutes
Cooking Time: 25 minutes
Servings: 4

Ingredients

- **For the Sourdough Tortilla Bowl:**
    - 1 cup sourdough discard
    - 1 ½ cups all-purpose flour
    - ¼ cup olive oil
    - ¼ teaspoon baking powder
    - ½ teaspoon salt
    - Warm water (as needed, about ⅓ cup)

- **For the Burrito Bowl Filling:**
    - 1 cup cooked rice (brown or white)
    - 1 can (15 oz) black beans, drained and rinsed
    - 1 cup corn kernels (fresh or frozen)
    - 1 red bell pepper, diced
    - 1 ripe avocado, sliced
    - 1 cup shredded lettuce
    - 1 cup diced tomatoes
    - ½ cup shredded cheese (optional)

- **For the Sourdough Salsa:**
    - 2 medium tomatoes, diced
    - 1 small onion, diced
    - 1 jalapeño pepper, minced (optional for spice)
    - ¼ cup chopped cilantro
    - Juice of 1 lime
    - Salt and pepper to taste

- **For Garnish:**
    - Sour cream
    - Chopped fresh cilantro
    - Lime wedges

Directions

1. **Prepare the Sourdough Tortilla Bowls:**
    - In a large mixing bowl, combine the sourdough discard, flour, olive oil, baking powder, and salt. Gradually add warm water and knead the dough until it forms a smooth, elastic ball. Cover with a damp cloth and let it rest for 10 minutes.
    - Divide the dough into 4 portions. Roll each portion into a 6-8 inch circle.
    - Heat a skillet over medium heat and cook each tortilla for 1-2 minutes on each side until slightly puffed and golden brown. Set aside to cool.

2. **Shape the Tortillas into Bowls:**
    - Preheat the oven to 375°F (190°C). Grease the underside of small oven-safe bowls or ramekins and drape each tortilla over the bowl. Gently

press to shape the tortilla into a bowl form.
- Bake for 10 minutes or until the edges are crisp. Remove and let them cool before filling.

3. **Prepare the Filling:**
   - In a large bowl, combine the cooked rice, black beans, corn, diced red bell pepper, and shredded lettuce. Mix well.

4. **Make the Sourdough Salsa:**
   - In a medium bowl, combine the diced tomatoes, onion, jalapeño, chopped cilantro, and lime juice. Season with salt and pepper to taste, stirring to blend flavors.

5. **Assemble the Burrito Bowls:**
   - Divide the rice and bean mixture evenly among the tortilla bowls. Add sliced avocado, diced tomatoes, and a sprinkle of shredded cheese (if using) on top of each bowl.
   - Spoon the sourdough salsa over each bowl, adding a dollop of sour cream, chopped cilantro, and a lime wedge for garnish.

Nutritional Values *(per serving)*

- Calories: 430
- Protein: 10g
- Carbohydrates: 55g
- Fat: 15g
- Fiber: 9g
- Sugars: 4g

Tips & Tricks

- **Adjusting Spice Levels:** For a mild flavor, omit the jalapeño in the salsa. For extra heat, consider adding cayenne or a dash of hot sauce.
- **Tortilla Bowl Alternatives:** If pressed for time, store-bought tortillas or pre-made taco shells can be used, although homemade offers a fresh, sourdough-enhanced flavor.
- **Adding Protein:** Grilled chicken, steak strips, or seasoned tofu can be added to the filling for a protein boost.
- **Storage:** Leftover filling ingredients can be stored separately in airtight containers for up to 3 days, making for an easy, quick meal prep option.

BBQ Chicken Flatbread

Preparation Time: 15 minutes
Cooking Time: 20 minutes
Servings: 4

Ingredients

- **For the Sourdough Flatbread:**
  - 1 cup sourdough discard
  - 1 ½ cups all-purpose flour
  - ¼ teaspoon baking powder
  - ½ teaspoon salt
  - ¼ cup olive oil
  - ⅓ cup warm water
- **For the Toppings:**

- 1 cup cooked chicken breast, shredded
- ½ cup barbecue sauce (plus extra for drizzling)
- 1 cup shredded mozzarella cheese
- ½ red onion, thinly sliced
- ¼ cup chopped cilantro
- 1 small green bell pepper, sliced

Directions

1. **Prepare the Sourdough Flatbread:**
   - In a large mixing bowl, combine the sourdough discard, flour, baking powder, salt, and olive oil. Slowly add warm water and knead the dough until it forms a smooth, pliable ball. Cover and let it rest for 10 minutes.
   - Divide the dough into two portions and roll each into a ¼-inch thick oval or round flatbread shape.
2. **Cook the Flatbread:**
   - Preheat a skillet or cast-iron pan over medium heat. Cook each flatbread for about 2-3 minutes per side until it is golden brown with light charring, creating a slightly crispy crust. Set aside to cool slightly.
3. **Assemble the Flatbread:**
   - Preheat the oven to 400°F (200°C). Spread a layer of barbecue sauce over each flatbread.
   - Top with shredded chicken, mozzarella cheese, red onion, and bell pepper slices.
4. **Bake the Flatbread:**
   - Place the assembled flatbreads on a baking sheet and bake for 10-12 minutes, or until the cheese is melted and bubbly.
5. **Garnish and Serve:**
   - Remove from the oven, sprinkle with chopped cilantro, and drizzle extra barbecue sauce on top. Slice and serve warm.

Nutritional Values *(per serving)*

- Calories: 380
- Protein: 22g
- Carbohydrates: 45g
- Fat: 14g
- Fiber: 3g
- Sugars: 8g

Tips & Tricks

- **Customizable Toppings:** Feel free to add other toppings, such as sliced mushrooms, pineapple for a sweet twist, or jalapeños for extra heat.
- **Using Store-Bought Flatbread:** In a pinch, store-bought flatbread can be used as a base, but homemade sourdough flatbread provides a richer, fresher flavor.

- **Marinate Chicken for Added Flavor:** Marinate the chicken in a bit of barbecue sauce before baking for deeper flavor.
- **Meal Prep Tip:** Cooked flatbread bases can be made in advance and refrigerated for up to 3 days or frozen for up to 1 month.

Savory Chicken Pot Pie

Preparation Time: 30 minutes
Cooking Time: 45 minutes
Servings: 6

Ingredients

- **For the Sourdough Crust:**
  - 1 cup sourdough discard
  - 1 ½ cups all-purpose flour
  - ½ teaspoon salt
  - ½ cup cold unsalted butter, cubed
  - ¼ cup ice water (or as needed)
- **For the Filling:**
  - 1 lb boneless, skinless chicken breasts, diced
  - 2 tablespoons olive oil
  - 1 medium onion, chopped
  - 2 medium carrots, diced
  - 1 cup frozen peas
  - 1 cup sliced mushrooms
  - 2 cloves garlic, minced
  - 1 teaspoon dried thyme
  - ½ teaspoon dried rosemary
  - Salt and pepper to taste
  - ¼ cup all-purpose flour
  - 2 cups chicken broth
  - ½ cup milk or cream

Directions

1. **Prepare the Sourdough Crust:**
   - In a food processor, pulse the flour and salt to combine. Add the cold butter cubes and pulse until the mixture resembles coarse crumbs.
   - Add the sourdough discard and pulse again. Gradually add ice water, 1 tablespoon at a time, until the dough begins to come together.
   - Shape the dough into a disk, wrap in plastic wrap, and refrigerate for at least 30 minutes.
2. **Prepare the Filling:**
   - In a large skillet, heat olive oil over medium heat. Add the diced chicken, season with salt and pepper, and cook until no longer pink, about 5-6 minutes. Remove the chicken and set it aside.
   - In the same skillet, add onions, carrots, peas, and mushrooms. Sauté for 5-6 minutes or until vegetables are tender. Add minced garlic, thyme, and rosemary, and cook for an additional 1-2 minutes.

- Sprinkle the flour over the vegetables and stir to coat. Gradually pour in the chicken broth and milk, stirring continuously until the mixture thickens, about 5 minutes.
- Return the cooked chicken to the skillet, stirring to combine. Adjust seasoning with salt and pepper if needed.

3. **Assemble the Pot Pie:**
   - Preheat the oven to 400°F (200°C). Transfer the filling mixture into a 9-inch pie dish or casserole dish.
   - Roll out the sourdough crust on a floured surface until it is large enough to cover the dish. Place the crust over the filling, trimming any excess and crimping the edges to seal.
   - Cut small slits in the crust to allow steam to escape.

4. **Bake the Pot Pie:**
   - Bake for 30-35 minutes, or until the crust is golden brown and the filling is bubbling. Allow the pie to rest for 10 minutes before serving.

Nutritional Values *(per serving)*

- Calories: 450
- Protein: 25g
- Carbohydrates: 40g
- Fat: 20g
- Fiber: 5g
- Sugars: 4g

Tips & Tricks

- **For a Flakier Crust:** Use very cold butter and avoid overworking the dough to ensure a tender, flaky crust.
- **Alternative Proteins:** Substitute chicken with turkey or make it vegetarian by adding more vegetables, such as potatoes and green beans.
- **Freezing Instructions:** Assemble the pot pie and freeze before baking for up to 3 months. Bake from frozen, adding an additional 10-15 minutes to the cooking time.
- **Reheating Tip:** For leftovers, reheat in the oven at 350°F (175°C) to keep the crust crisp.

Sourdough Pierogi

Preparation Time: 45 minutes
Cooking Time: 30 minutes
Servings: 6 (makes about 24 pierogi)

Ingredients

- **For the Dough:**
  - 1 cup sourdough discard
  - 2 cups all-purpose flour (plus more for dusting)
  - ½ teaspoon salt
  - 2 large eggs
  - ¼ cup water (or as needed)
- **For the Filling:**
  - 1 lb potatoes, peeled and diced
  - 1 cup shredded cheddar cheese

- ¼ cup sour cream
- 2 tablespoons unsalted butter
- Salt and pepper to taste
- **For Serving:**
    - 2 tablespoons butter, melted
    - Chopped chives or green onions
    - Sour cream (optional)

Directions

1. **Prepare the Pierogi Dough:**
    - In a large mixing bowl, combine the sourdough discard, flour, and salt. Add the eggs and water, mixing until a rough dough forms.
    - Turn the dough onto a floured surface and knead for about 5-7 minutes until smooth and elastic. Cover with a damp towel and let it rest for 15 minutes.
2. **Prepare the Filling:**
    - Boil the potatoes in a pot of salted water until tender, about 10-12 minutes. Drain and return to the pot.
    - Mash the potatoes with cheddar cheese, sour cream, and butter until smooth. Season with salt and pepper to taste. Allow the filling to cool slightly before assembling the pierogi.
3. **Assemble the Pierogi:**
    - Roll out the dough on a floured surface to about ⅛-inch thickness. Use a 3-inch round cutter (or a glass) to cut out circles from the dough.
    - Place about 1 tablespoon of filling in the center of each dough circle. Fold the dough over the filling to form a half-moon shape, pressing the edges to seal. Use a fork to crimp the edges and ensure they are fully sealed.
4. **Cook the Pierogi:**
    - Bring a large pot of salted water to a gentle boil. Drop the pierogi in batches, cooking until they float to the top, about 3-4 minutes. Remove with a slotted spoon and set aside.
5. **Finish and Serve:**
    - In a large skillet, melt 2 tablespoons of butter over medium heat. Add the boiled pierogi and cook until golden brown on each side, about 2-3 minutes per side.
    - Garnish with chopped chives or green onions and serve with sour cream, if desired.

Nutritional Values *(per serving)*

- Calories: 320
- Protein: 10g
- Carbohydrates: 45g
- Fat: 12g
- Fiber: 3g

- Sugars: 1g

Tips & Tricks

- **Make-Ahead Option:** The pierogi can be made ahead and frozen before boiling. Freeze in a single layer on a baking sheet, then transfer to a freezer bag once solid.
- **Flavor Variations:** Try adding caramelized onions or sautéed mushrooms to the filling for extra flavor.
- **Alternative Filling Ideas:** Cottage cheese, ground meat, or even sauerkraut can be used as filling for a unique twist on traditional pierogi.
- **Reheating:** To reheat, warm the pierogi in a skillet with a little butter until heated through and crisp.

Stromboli with Italian Herbs

Preparation Time: 30 minutes
Cooking Time: 30 minutes
Servings: 4-6

Ingredients

- **For the Dough:**
    - 1 cup sourdough discard
    - 2 ½ cups all-purpose flour
    - 1 teaspoon salt
    - 1 teaspoon sugar
    - 1 teaspoon dried Italian herbs (basil, oregano, thyme)
    - 1 tablespoon olive oil
    - ¾ cup warm water (adjust as needed)
- **For the Filling:**
    - ½ cup marinara sauce
    - 1 cup shredded mozzarella cheese
    - ¼ cup grated Parmesan cheese
    - ½ cup sliced pepperoni (or any preferred deli meat)
    - ½ cup sautéed mushrooms (optional)
    - ¼ cup sliced bell peppers
    - 1 tablespoon chopped fresh basil or parsley (optional)
- **For Brushing:**
    - 1 egg, beaten (for egg wash)
    - 1 teaspoon dried Italian herbs (for garnish)

Directions

1. **Prepare the Dough:**
    - In a large mixing bowl, combine the sourdough discard, flour, salt, sugar, Italian herbs, and olive oil. Gradually add warm water while mixing, until a smooth dough forms.
    - Knead the dough on a floured surface for about 5-7 minutes, until elastic. Cover and let rest for 15-20 minutes.
2. **Roll Out the Dough:**
    - Preheat the oven to 400°F (200°C) and line a baking sheet with parchment paper.
    - Roll the dough out on a floured surface into a

rectangle about 12x15 inches in size.

3. **Add the Filling:**
   - Spread a thin layer of marinara sauce over the dough, leaving a 1-inch border around the edges.
   - Sprinkle the mozzarella and Parmesan cheese evenly over the sauce. Layer with pepperoni, sautéed mushrooms, and bell peppers. Sprinkle chopped fresh basil or parsley for extra flavor, if desired.

4. **Roll and Seal the Stromboli:**
   - Starting from one of the long sides, carefully roll the dough into a tight log. Pinch the edges and ends to seal completely.
   - Place the rolled stromboli on the prepared baking sheet, seam side down.

5. **Apply Egg Wash and Bake:**
   - Brush the top with beaten egg and sprinkle with dried Italian herbs. Use a sharp knife to cut small slits on top to allow steam to escape.
   - Bake for 25-30 minutes, or until golden brown and cooked through.

6. **Slice and Serve:**
   - Allow the stromboli to cool for about 5 minutes before slicing. Serve with extra marinara sauce for dipping, if desired.

Nutritional Values *(per serving)*

- Calories: 410
- Protein: 15g
- Carbohydrates: 50g
- Fat: 18g
- Fiber: 3g
- Sugars: 4g

Tips & Tricks

- **Customizing Fillings:** Substitute or add ingredients like spinach, ham, or olives for a personalized touch.
- **For Extra Crispness:** Brush the crust with olive oil before baking to enhance its golden, crispy texture.
- **Storage and Reheating:** Leftovers can be wrapped and stored in the refrigerator for up to 3 days. Reheat in the oven at 350°F (175°C) to maintain crispness.
- **Freezing Option:** To freeze, prepare the stromboli through the rolling step and freeze before baking. Thaw and bake when ready.

Discard Gnocchi

Preparation Time: 30 minutes
Cooking Time: 10 minutes
Servings: 4

Ingredients

- **For the Gnocchi:**
  - 1 cup sourdough discard

- 1 ½ cups all-purpose flour (plus more for dusting)
- 1 cup ricotta cheese
- ½ cup grated Parmesan cheese
- 1 large egg
- Salt and pepper to taste

- **For the Sauce (Optional):**
  - 2 tablespoons unsalted butter
  - 2 cloves garlic, minced
  - ¼ cup heavy cream
  - ¼ cup grated Parmesan cheese
  - Freshly chopped basil or parsley for garnish

Directions

1. **Prepare the Gnocchi Dough:**
   - In a large mixing bowl, combine the sourdough discard, flour, ricotta cheese, Parmesan, egg, salt, and pepper. Mix until a soft dough forms. Avoid over-mixing, as this will make the gnocchi tough.
   - Turn the dough onto a floured surface and gently knead until it's smooth and no longer sticky. Divide the dough into four portions.

2. **Shape the Gnocchi:**
   - Roll each portion into a long rope, about ½ inch in diameter. Use a knife to cut the rope into 1-inch pieces.
   - For a classic gnocchi texture, gently press each piece against the tines of a fork to create ridges. This helps the sauce adhere to the gnocchi.

3. **Cook the Gnocchi:**
   - Bring a large pot of salted water to a boil. Drop the gnocchi in batches, cooking until they float to the surface, about 2-3 minutes. Use a slotted spoon to remove the gnocchi and set aside.

4. **Prepare the Sauce (Optional):**
   - In a large skillet, melt the butter over medium heat. Add minced garlic and sauté until fragrant, about 1 minute.
   - Stir in the heavy cream and grated Parmesan, cooking until the sauce is smooth and slightly thickened, about 2-3 minutes.

5. **Combine and Serve:**
   - Add the cooked gnocchi to the skillet with the sauce, tossing to coat evenly. Serve warm, garnished with fresh basil or parsley if desired.

Nutritional Values *(per serving)*

- Calories: 360
- Protein: 15g
- Carbohydrates: 45g
- Fat: 12g
- Fiber: 2g
- Sugars: 1g

Tips & Tricks

- **For a Crispy Texture:** After boiling, sauté the gnocchi in a skillet with a little olive oil until golden brown on each side.
- **Freezing Gnocchi:** Arrange uncooked gnocchi on a baking sheet, freeze until solid, and transfer to a freezer bag. Cook from frozen, adding a few extra minutes.
- **Alternative Sauces:** Try serving gnocchi with a marinara sauce or a pesto for different flavor profiles.
- **Adding Vegetables:** Toss in sautéed spinach or roasted cherry tomatoes to add color and nutrients.

Stromboli with Italian Herbs

Preparation Time: 30 minutes
Cooking Time: 30 minutes
Servings: 4-6

Ingredients

- **For the Dough:**
  - 1 cup sourdough discard
  - 2 ½ cups all-purpose flour
  - 1 teaspoon salt
  - 1 teaspoon sugar
  - 1 teaspoon dried Italian herbs (basil, oregano, thyme)
  - 1 tablespoon olive oil
  - ¾ cup warm water (adjust as needed)
- **For the Filling:**
  - ½ cup marinara sauce
  - 1 cup shredded mozzarella cheese
  - ¼ cup grated Parmesan cheese
  - ½ cup sliced pepperoni (or any preferred deli meat)
  - ½ cup sautéed mushrooms (optional)
  - ¼ cup sliced bell peppers
  - 1 tablespoon chopped fresh basil or parsley (optional)
- **For Brushing:**
  - 1 egg, beaten (for egg wash)
  - 1 teaspoon dried Italian herbs (for garnish)

Directions

1. **Prepare the Dough:**
   - In a large mixing bowl, combine the sourdough discard, flour, salt, sugar, Italian herbs, and olive oil. Gradually add warm water while mixing until a smooth dough forms.
   - Knead the dough on a floured surface for about 5-7 minutes, until elastic. Cover and let rest for 15-20 minutes.
2. **Roll Out the Dough:**
   - Preheat the oven to 400°F (200°C) and line a baking sheet with parchment paper.
   - Roll the dough out on a floured surface into a

rectangle about 12x15 inches in size.

3. **Add the Filling:**
   - Spread a thin layer of marinara sauce over the dough, leaving a 1-inch border around the edges.
   - Sprinkle the mozzarella and Parmesan cheese evenly over the sauce. Layer with pepperoni, sautéed mushrooms, and bell peppers. Sprinkle chopped fresh basil or parsley for extra flavor if desired.

4. **Roll and Seal the Stromboli:**
   - Starting from one of the long sides, carefully roll the dough into a tight log. Pinch the edges and ends to seal completely.
   - Place the rolled stromboli on the prepared baking sheet, seam side down.

5. **Apply Egg Wash and Bake:**
   - Brush the top with beaten egg and sprinkle with dried Italian herbs. Use a sharp knife to cut small slits on top to allow steam to escape.
   - Bake for 25-30 minutes, or until golden brown and cooked through.

6. **Slice and Serve:**
   - Allow the stromboli to cool for about 5 minutes before slicing. Serve with extra marinara sauce for dipping, if desired.

Nutritional Values *(per serving)*

- Calories: 410
- Protein: 15g
- Carbohydrates: 50g
- Fat: 18g
- Fiber: 3g
- Sugars: 4g

Tips & Tricks

- **Customizing Fillings:** Substitute or add ingredients like spinach, ham, or olives for a personalized touch.
- **For Extra Crispness:** Brush the crust with olive oil before baking to enhance its golden, crispy texture.
- **Storage and Reheating:** Leftovers can be wrapped and stored in the refrigerator for up to 3 days. Reheat in the oven at 350°F (175°C) to maintain crispness.
- **Freezing Option:** To freeze, prepare the stromboli through the rolling step and freeze before baking. Thaw and bake when ready.

Creamy Alfredo Pasta with Sourdough

Preparation Time: 15 minutes
Cooking Time: 20 minutes
Servings: 4

Ingredients

- **For the Sourdough Pasta:**
  - 1 cup sourdough discard

- 1 ½ cups all-purpose flour
- 2 large eggs
- ½ teaspoon salt
- **For the Alfredo Sauce:**
  - 3 tablespoons unsalted butter
  - 3 cloves garlic, minced
  - 1 ½ cups heavy cream
  - 1 cup grated Parmesan cheese
  - Salt and pepper to taste
  - Chopped parsley for garnish

Directions

1. **Prepare the Sourdough Pasta:**
   - In a bowl, mix sourdough discard, flour, eggs, and salt until a dough forms. Knead on a floured surface for 5-7 minutes until smooth. Cover and rest for 20 minutes.
   - Roll the dough out into thin sheets and cut into desired pasta shapes (fettuccine or linguine).
2. **Cook the Pasta:**
   - Bring a large pot of salted water to a boil. Add pasta and cook for 2-3 minutes until tender. Drain and set aside.
3. **Make the Alfredo Sauce:**
   - In a skillet, melt butter over medium heat. Add garlic and sauté until fragrant.
   - Stir in heavy cream, then add Parmesan, whisking until smooth. Season with salt and pepper.
4. **Combine and Serve:**
   - Add pasta to the sauce, tossing to coat. Garnish with chopped parsley.

Nutritional Values *(per serving)*

- Calories: 610
- Protein: 18g
- Carbohydrates: 45g
- Fat: 40g
- Fiber: 2g
- Sugars: 1g

Tips & Tricks

- **For Extra Flavor:** Add sautéed mushrooms or grilled chicken to the pasta.
- **Using Store-Bought Pasta:** Substitute with 8 oz store-bought pasta if preferred.
- **Storing Leftovers:** Keep refrigerated for up to 2 days; reheat with a splash of milk.

Recipe 8: Vegetarian Lasagna with Sourdough Crust

Preparation Time: 40 minutes
Cooking Time: 1 hour
Servings: 6-8

Ingredients

- **For the Sourdough Crust:**
  - 1 cup sourdough discard
  - 1 ½ cups all-purpose flour

- ½ teaspoon salt
- ½ cup cold butter, cubed
- ¼ cup ice water
- **For the Filling:**
  - 2 cups ricotta cheese
  - 2 cups shredded mozzarella cheese
  - 1 cup grated Parmesan cheese
  - 1 large zucchini, sliced
  - 1 large eggplant, sliced
  - 1 cup spinach leaves
  - 2 cups marinara sauce

Directions

1. **Prepare the Sourdough Crust:**
   - Mix sourdough discard, flour, and salt. Add cold butter, pulse to crumbs. Add ice water until dough forms.
   - Chill dough for 30 minutes, roll into a 9x13-inch dish base.
2. **Assemble Lasagna Layers:**
   - Spread marinara, layer zucchini, eggplant, ricotta, and cheeses, repeat until ingredients are used.
3. **Bake:**
   - Cover with foil, bake at 375°F (190°C) for 45 minutes. Uncover, bake another 15 minutes.

Nutritional Values *(per serving)*

- Calories: 530
- Protein: 20g
- Carbohydrates: 35g
- Fat: 35g
- Fiber: 5g

Tips & Tricks

- **Add Fresh Herbs:** Try basil or oregano.
- **Make-Ahead:** Assembled lasagna can be refrigerated for 1 day before baking.

Recipe 9: Ravioli with Spinach Filling

Preparation Time: 45 minutes
Cooking Time: 10 minutes
Servings: 4

Ingredients

- **For the Dough:**
  - 1 cup sourdough discard
  - 1 ½ cups all-purpose flour (plus more for dusting)
  - 2 large eggs
  - ½ teaspoon salt
- **For the Filling:**
  - 1 cup ricotta cheese
  - 1 cup fresh spinach, finely chopped
  - ½ cup grated Parmesan cheese
  - Salt and pepper to taste
  - ¼ teaspoon nutmeg (optional)
- **For the Sauce (Optional):**
  - 2 tablespoons unsalted butter

- 2 cloves garlic, minced
- ½ cup heavy cream
- Salt and pepper to taste
- Freshly grated Parmesan and chopped parsley for garnish

Directions

1. **Prepare the Dough:**
    - In a large mixing bowl, combine the sourdough discard, flour, eggs, and salt. Mix until a dough forms.
    - Turn the dough onto a floured surface and knead for 5-7 minutes, or until smooth and elastic. Cover and let it rest for 15 minutes.

2. **Prepare the Filling:**
    - In a medium bowl, combine the ricotta cheese, chopped spinach, Parmesan, salt, pepper, and nutmeg (if using). Mix until well-blended. Set aside.

3. **Assemble the Ravioli:**
    - Roll out the dough on a floured surface until very thin, about ⅛ inch thick.
    - Cut the dough into 2-inch squares or rounds. Place 1 teaspoon of filling in the center of each piece.
    - Moisten the edges with a little water, then place another piece of dough on top, pressing firmly to seal. Use a fork to crimp the edges.

4. **Cook the Ravioli:**
    - Bring a large pot of salted water to a gentle boil. Add the ravioli in batches and cook for 2-3 minutes, or until they float to the surface. Use a slotted spoon to remove the ravioli and set aside.

5. **Prepare the Sauce (Optional):**
    - In a large skillet, melt the butter over medium heat. Add minced garlic and sauté until fragrant, about 1 minute.
    - Stir in the heavy cream, then season with salt and pepper to taste. Simmer for 2-3 minutes, or until slightly thickened.

6. **Combine and Serve:**
    - Add the cooked ravioli to the skillet with the sauce, tossing gently to coat. Garnish with freshly grated Parmesan and chopped parsley before serving.

Nutritional Values *(per serving)*

- Calories: 380
- Protein: 15g
- Carbohydrates: 45g
- Fat: 15g
- Fiber: 2g
- Sugars: 1g

Tips & Tricks

- **Freezing Ravioli:** Lay uncooked ravioli on a baking sheet in a single layer, freeze, then transfer to a

freezer bag. Cook directly from frozen, adding an extra 1-2 minutes.
- **Flavor Variations:** Add chopped basil or sun-dried tomatoes to the filling for an extra burst of flavor.
- **Make-Ahead Option:** The filling and dough can be prepared a day ahead and stored separately in the refrigerator.

Veggie Burgers with Sourdough Buns

Preparation Time: 20 minutes
Cooking Time: 15 minutes
Servings: 4

Ingredients

- **For the Sourdough Buns:**
    - 1 cup sourdough discard
    - 1 ½ cups all-purpose flour
    - 1 tablespoon olive oil
    - ½ teaspoon salt
    - ½ cup warm water
- **For the Veggie Patties:**
    - 1 cup cooked quinoa
    - 1 can (15 oz) black beans, drained and mashed
    - 1 carrot, grated
    - ½ cup breadcrumbs
    - 2 tablespoons chopped fresh parsley
    - Salt and pepper to taste
    - Olive oil for frying
- **For Toppings:**
    - Lettuce leaves
    - Sliced tomato
    - Sliced red onion
    - Sliced avocado (optional)
    - Ketchup or preferred condiments

Directions

1. **Prepare the Sourdough Buns:**
    - In a large bowl, combine sourdough discard, flour, olive oil, salt, and warm water. Knead until smooth and elastic.
    - Divide into 4 balls, shape each into a bun, and place on a baking sheet. Allow to rest for 15 minutes.
    - Bake at 375°F (190°C) for 12-15 minutes until golden brown.
2. **Prepare the Veggie Patties:**
    - In a mixing bowl, combine quinoa, mashed black beans, grated carrot, breadcrumbs, parsley, salt, and pepper. Form into 4 patties.
    - In a skillet, heat olive oil over medium heat. Cook each patty for 3-4 minutes per side, until golden brown.
3. **Assemble the Burgers:**
    - Slice the buns in half. Layer each bun with a veggie patty, lettuce, tomato, onion, and avocado (if using). Add condiments as desired.

Nutritional Values *(per serving)*

- Calories: 420
- Protein: 14g
- Carbohydrates: 55g
- Fat: 14g
- Fiber: 8g
- Sugars: 3g

Tips & Tricks

- **Customizing the Patties:** Add spices like cumin or smoked paprika to the patties for extra flavor.
- **Meal Prep Option:** Patties can be made in advance and frozen for up to 1 month.
- **Gluten-Free Option:** Use gluten-free breadcrumbs and flour.

Calzones with Mixed Cheese

Preparation Time: 30 minutes
Cooking Time: 20 minutes
Servings: 4

Ingredients

- **For the Dough:**
    - 1 cup sourdough discard
    - 1 ½ cups all-purpose flour
    - ½ teaspoon salt
    - 1 tablespoon olive oil
    - ⅓ cup warm water
- **For the Filling:**
    - 1 cup ricotta cheese
    - 1 cup shredded mozzarella cheese
    - ½ cup grated Parmesan cheese
    - ½ cup sautéed spinach (optional)
    - Salt and pepper to taste

Directions

1. **Prepare the Dough:**
    - Mix sourdough discard, flour, salt, olive oil, and warm water until a smooth dough forms.
    - Divide dough into four balls and roll each into a 6-inch circle.
2. **Assemble the Calzones:**
    - Place a portion of filling on half of each dough circle, then fold over and seal edges.
    - Brush with olive oil and bake at 400°F (200°C) for 15-20 minutes until golden brown.

Nutritional Values *(per serving)*

- Calories: 450
- Protein: 18g
- Carbohydrates: 52g
- Fat: 18g

Tips & Tricks

- **Adding Meat:** For a heartier calzone, add pepperoni or sausage to the filling.
- **Make-Ahead:** Assembled calzones can be frozen before baking; bake from frozen with 5 extra minutes.

Cheesy Enchiladas

Preparation Time: 20 minutes
Cooking Time: 25 minutes
Servings: 4

Ingredients

- **For the Sourdough Tortillas:**
    - 1 cup sourdough discard
    - 1 ½ cups all-purpose flour
    - ½ teaspoon salt
    - 2 tablespoons olive oil
    - ½ cup warm water
- **For the Enchilada Filling:**
    - 1 ½ cups shredded cheddar cheese
    - 1 cup shredded Monterey Jack cheese
    - 1 can (15 oz) black beans, drained and rinsed
    - ½ cup corn kernels
    - 1 small onion, diced
    - 1 teaspoon ground cumin
    - Salt and pepper to taste
- **For the Enchilada Sauce:**
    - 1 can (15 oz) tomato sauce
    - 1 teaspoon chili powder
    - ½ teaspoon garlic powder
    - ½ teaspoon onion powder
    - Salt and pepper to taste
- **For Garnish:**
    - Chopped cilantro
    - Sour cream (optional)

Directions

1. **Prepare the Sourdough Tortillas:**
    - In a mixing bowl, combine sourdough discard, flour, salt, olive oil, and warm water. Knead until smooth.
    - Divide dough into 8 balls, roll each into a thin circle.
    - Cook each tortilla on a hot skillet for 1-2 minutes per side. Set aside.
2. **Prepare the Enchilada Filling:**
    - In a bowl, mix cheddar cheese, Monterey Jack, black beans, corn, diced onion, cumin, salt, and pepper.
3. **Assemble the Enchiladas:**
    - Preheat oven to 375°F (190°C). Pour a small amount of enchilada sauce into a 9x13-inch baking dish.
    - Place filling in each tortilla, roll tightly, and arrange in the dish seam-side down. Pour remaining sauce over the top and sprinkle with extra cheese.
4. **Bake the Enchiladas:**
    - Bake for 20-25 minutes, or until bubbly and golden. Garnish with chopped cilantro and sour cream, if desired.

Nutritional Values *(per serving)*

- Calories: 480

- Protein: 18g
- Carbohydrates: 56g
- Fat: 22g
- Fiber: 8g

Tips & Tricks

- **Customize the Filling:** Add cooked chicken or beef for a heartier option.
- **Make-Ahead:** Assemble the enchiladas and refrigerate overnight; bake before serving.
- **Spice it Up:** Add jalapeños or a dash of hot sauce to the sauce for extra heat.

Fish Tacos with Sourdough Tortillas

Preparation Time: 15 minutes
Cooking Time: 10 minutes
Servings: 4

Ingredients

- **For the Sourdough Tortillas:**
    - 1 cup sourdough discard
    - 1 ½ cups all-purpose flour
    - ½ teaspoon salt
    - 2 tablespoons olive oil
    - ½ cup warm water
- **For the Fish and Toppings:**
    - 1 lb white fish fillets (e.g., cod or tilapia), cut into strips
    - 1 teaspoon chili powder
    - Salt and pepper to taste
    - 2 tablespoons olive oil
    - Shredded cabbage
    - Sliced avocado
    - Lime wedges
    - Chopped cilantro

Directions

1. **Prepare the Sourdough Tortillas:**
    - Combine sourdough discard, flour, salt, olive oil, and warm water in a bowl. Knead until smooth, then divide into 8 balls.
    - Roll each ball into a thin circle, cook on a hot skillet for 1-2 minutes per side.
2. **Cook the Fish:**
    - Season fish with chili powder, salt, and pepper. Heat olive oil in a skillet over medium-high heat and cook fish for 3-4 minutes per side.
3. **Assemble the Tacos:**
    - Place fish on each tortilla, top with cabbage, avocado, cilantro, and a squeeze of lime.

Nutritional Values (*per serving*)

- Calories: 370
- Protein: 28g
- Carbohydrates: 40g
- Fat: 10g
- Fiber: 6g

Tips & Tricks

- **Topping Ideas:** Add salsa, sour cream, or hot sauce for added flavor.
- **Make-Ahead Tortillas:** Tortillas can be made in advance and kept warm wrapped in a cloth.
- **Alternative Fish:** Shrimp or salmon can be used instead of white fish.

Meatball Subs on Sourdough Hoagies

Preparation Time: 25 minutes
Cooking Time: 20 minutes
Servings: 4

Ingredients

- **For the Sourdough Hoagie Rolls:**
    - 1 cup sourdough discard
    - 2 cups all-purpose flour
    - 1 tablespoon olive oil
    - 1 teaspoon salt
    - ¾ cup warm water
- **For the Meatballs:**
    - 1 lb ground beef
    - ½ cup breadcrumbs
    - 1 egg
    - 2 cloves garlic, minced
    - ¼ cup grated Parmesan cheese
    - Salt and pepper to taste
- **For Assembly:**
    - 1 cup marinara sauce
    - 1 cup shredded mozzarella cheese
    - Fresh basil for garnish

Directions

1. **Prepare the Hoagie Rolls:**
    - In a bowl, mix sourdough discard, flour, olive oil, salt, and water. Knead until smooth, divide into 4 rolls, and let rest for 15 minutes.
    - Bake at 375°F (190°C) for 15-18 minutes.
2. **Prepare the Meatballs:**
    - Mix beef, breadcrumbs, egg, garlic, Parmesan, salt, and pepper. Form into 1-inch balls.
    - Brown meatballs in a skillet, then simmer in marinara sauce for 10 minutes.
3. **Assemble the Subs:**
    - Cut hoagie rolls in half, place meatballs and sauce, top with mozzarella. Broil until cheese melts. Garnish with basil.

Nutritional Values *(per serving)*

- Calories: 520
- Protein: 32g
- Carbohydrates: 45g
- Fat: 22g
- Fiber: 3g

Tips & Tricks

- **Alternative Cheese:** Use provolone or Parmesan for added flavor.
- **Make-Ahead:** Meatballs can be prepared in advance and refrigerated.
- **Spice It Up:** Add crushed red pepper for a kick.

Tomato Basil Sourdough Pasta

Preparation Time: 20 minutes
Cooking Time: 15 minutes
Servings: 4

Ingredients

- **For the Sourdough Pasta:**
  - 1 cup sourdough discard
  - 1 ½ cups all-purpose flour
  - 2 large eggs
  - ½ teaspoon salt
- **For the Sauce:**
  - 2 tablespoons olive oil
  - 3 cloves garlic, minced
  - 2 cups cherry tomatoes, halved
  - ½ cup fresh basil leaves, chopped
  - Salt and pepper to taste
  - Grated Parmesan for garnish

Directions

1. **Prepare the Sourdough Pasta:**
   - In a bowl, combine sourdough discard, flour, eggs, and salt. Knead for 5 minutes until smooth. Let rest for 15 minutes.
   - Roll into thin sheets, cut into fettuccine.
2. **Cook the Pasta:**
   - Boil salted water, add pasta, cook for 2-3 minutes. Drain.
3. **Prepare the Sauce:**
   - Heat olive oil in a skillet, sauté garlic, add tomatoes. Cook until softened.
   - Add basil, salt, pepper, and toss pasta in sauce.

Nutritional Values *(per serving)*

- Calories: 450
- Protein: 15g
- Carbohydrates: 50g
- Fat: 15g
- Fiber: 4g

Tips & Tricks

- **Add Protein:** Sautéed shrimp or grilled chicken pairs well.
- **Make-Ahead Sauce:** The sauce can be made ahead and refrigerated.
- **Fresh Herbs:** Garnish with fresh parsley or thyme for extra flavor.

CHAPTER 5: DELECTABLE DESSERTS

Classic Brownies with a Sourdough Twist

Preparation Time: 15 minutes
Cooking Time: 30 minutes
Servings: 12 brownies

Ingredients:

- 1/2 cup sourdough discard
- 1/2 cup all-purpose flour
- 1/2 cup unsweetened cocoa powder
- 1/2 teaspoon baking powder
- 1/4 teaspoon salt
- 1/2 cup unsalted butter, melted
- 1 cup granulated sugar
- 1/2 cup brown sugar, packed
- 2 large eggs
- 1 teaspoon vanilla extract
- 1/2 cup chocolate chips (optional)

Directions:

1. **Preheat and Prepare Pan:** Preheat the oven to 350°F (175°C). Grease an 8x8-inch baking pan or line it with parchment paper for easy removal.
2. **Combine Dry Ingredients:** In a medium bowl, whisk together the flour, cocoa powder, baking powder, and salt.
3. **Mix Wet Ingredients:** In a separate bowl, combine the melted butter, granulated sugar, and brown sugar. Whisk until smooth, then add the eggs and vanilla extract, stirring until well blended.
4. **Add Sourdough Discard:** Stir in the sourdough discard until fully incorporated.
5. **Combine Wet and Dry Mixtures:** Gradually add the dry ingredients to the wet mixture, stirring until just combined. Fold in the chocolate chips if desired.
6. **Bake:** Pour the batter into the prepared pan, spreading it evenly. Bake for 30-35 minutes or until a toothpick inserted in the center comes out with a few moist crumbs.
7. **Cool and Serve:** Allow the brownies to cool in the pan before slicing.

Nutritional Values (per serving):

- **Calories:** 210
- **Carbohydrates:** 27g
- **Protein:** 2g
- **Fat:** 10g
- **Fiber:** 2g

Tips & Tricks:

- For an extra chocolatey flavor, add a handful of chocolate chunks.
- Use espresso powder for a deeper chocolate taste.
- Store brownies in an airtight container for up to a week at room temperature.

Apple Cinnamon Fritters

Preparation Time: 20 minutes
Cooking Time: 15 minutes
Servings: 12 fritters

Ingredients:

- 1/2 cup sourdough discard
- 1 cup all-purpose flour
- 1/4 cup granulated sugar
- 1 teaspoon baking powder
- 1/2 teaspoon cinnamon
- 1/4 teaspoon salt
- 1/4 cup milk
- 1 large egg
- 1 cup diced apple
- Vegetable oil, for frying
- Powdered sugar, for dusting

Directions:

1. **Prepare Batter:** In a large bowl, whisk together the flour, sugar, baking powder, cinnamon, and salt.
2. **Mix Wet Ingredients:** In a separate bowl, combine the sourdough discard, milk, and egg. Mix until smooth.
3. **Combine and Fold in Apples:** Pour the wet ingredients into the dry ingredients, stirring until just combined. Gently fold in the diced apples.
4. **Heat Oil and Fry:** In a deep skillet, heat about 1 inch of vegetable oil to 350°F (175°C). Drop spoonfuls of batter into the hot oil, frying until golden brown on each side (about 2-3 minutes per side).
5. **Drain and Dust:** Use a slotted spoon to remove the fritters and drain on paper towels. Dust with powdered sugar before serving.

Nutritional Values (per serving):

- **Calories:** 120
- **Carbohydrates:** 18g
- **Protein:** 2g
- **Fat:** 5g
- **Fiber:** 1g

Tips & Tricks:

- Serve warm for the best flavor.
- For extra sweetness, drizzle with a glaze made from powdered sugar and milk.
- Use a firm apple variety like Granny Smith for a tart contrast.

Banana Cream Pie

Preparation Time: 25 minutes
Chilling Time: 4 hours
Servings: 8 slices

Ingredients:

- **For the crust:**
    - 1/2 cup sourdough discard
    - 1 1/4 cups all-purpose flour
    - 1/4 teaspoon salt
    - 1/2 cup cold unsalted butter, cubed
    - 3-4 tablespoons ice water
- **For the filling:**
    - 1/2 cup granulated sugar
    - 1/4 cup cornstarch

- - 1/4 teaspoon salt
  - 2 cups whole milk
  - 3 large egg yolks
  - 2 tablespoons unsalted butter
  - 1 teaspoon vanilla extract
  - 3 large ripe bananas, sliced
- **For topping:** Whipped cream

Directions:

1. **Prepare Crust:** In a large bowl, combine flour and salt. Cut in the butter until mixture resembles coarse crumbs. Add the sourdough discard and ice water, mixing until dough forms. Roll out and press into a pie dish, then bake at 350°F (175°C) for 10-12 minutes or until golden. Cool.
2. **Make the Filling:** In a medium saucepan, combine sugar, cornstarch, and salt. Gradually whisk in milk, cooking over medium heat until thickened (about 5-7 minutes). Remove from heat.
3. **Add Egg Yolks and Butter:** Temper the egg yolks by adding a small amount of the hot mixture, then whisk them back into the pan. Stir in butter and vanilla.
4. **Assemble Pie:** Layer the sliced bananas over the crust, pour the custard over the bananas, and smooth the top. Refrigerate for at least 4 hours.
5. **Serve:** Top with whipped cream before serving.

Nutritional Values (per serving):

- **Calories:** 290
- **Carbohydrates:** 35g
- **Protein:** 4g
- **Fat:** 14g
- **Fiber:** 2g

Tips & Tricks:

- For a firmer crust, pre-bake with pie weights.
- Chill thoroughly to allow custard to set properly.
- Use homemade whipped cream for the freshest flavor.

Rich Chocolate Babka

Preparation Time: 30 minutes (plus 2 hours for rising)
Cooking Time: 45 minutes
Servings: 1 loaf

Ingredients:

- **Dough:**
  - 1/2 cup sourdough discard
  - 2 1/4 cups all-purpose flour
  - 1/4 cup granulated sugar
  - 1/4 teaspoon salt
  - 1/2 cup milk, warmed
  - 1 large egg
  - 1/4 cup unsalted butter, softened
- **Filling:**
  - 1/2 cup dark chocolate, chopped
  - 1/4 cup unsalted butter

- 1/4 cup granulated sugar
- 2 tablespoons cocoa powder
- **Topping:**
  - 2 tablespoons granulated sugar
  - 1 tablespoon water

Directions:

1. **Prepare the Dough:** In a large mixing bowl, combine flour, sugar, and salt. In a separate bowl, mix sourdough discard, warm milk, and egg. Gradually add the wet ingredients to the dry mixture, then knead in the softened butter until dough is smooth. Cover and let rise for 1-2 hours.

2. **Make the Filling:** In a small saucepan, melt the chocolate and butter over low heat. Stir in sugar and cocoa powder, mixing until smooth. Let cool slightly.

3. **Assemble the Babka:** Roll the dough into a rectangle. Spread the filling evenly over the dough, then roll up tightly from the short side. Cut the roll in half lengthwise, twist the halves together, and place in a greased loaf pan.

4. **Second Rise and Bake:** Let the assembled babka rise for 1 hour. Preheat oven to 350°F (175°C) and bake for 40-45 minutes, until golden brown.

5. **Add Topping:** In a small saucepan, heat the sugar and water until dissolved. Brush over the warm babka.

Nutritional Values (per serving):

- **Calories:** 250
- **Carbohydrates:** 32g
- **Protein:** 4g
- **Fat:** 12g
- **Fiber:** 2g

Tips & Tricks:

- For an extra twist, add a sprinkle of cinnamon to the filling.
- Ensure the filling has cooled slightly before spreading to prevent melting the dough.
- Babka can be stored in an airtight container for up to 3 days.

Gingerbread Cookies

Preparation Time: 20 minutes
Chilling Time: 1 hour
Cooking Time: 10 minutes
Servings: 24 cookies

Ingredients:

- 1/4 cup sourdough discard
- 1/2 cup unsalted butter, softened
- 1/2 cup brown sugar, packed
- 1/2 cup molasses
- 1 large egg
- 2 1/2 cups all-purpose flour
- 1 teaspoon baking soda
- 1 tablespoon ground ginger
- 1 teaspoon cinnamon
- 1/4 teaspoon cloves
- 1/4 teaspoon nutmeg

- Pinch of salt

Directions:

1. **Prepare the Dough:** In a mixing bowl, cream together butter, brown sugar, and molasses until fluffy. Add the egg and sourdough discard, mixing until smooth.

2. **Combine Dry Ingredients:** In a separate bowl, whisk together flour, baking soda, spices, and salt. Gradually add the dry ingredients to the wet mixture, mixing until a dough forms.

3. **Chill Dough:** Wrap the dough in plastic wrap and chill for 1 hour.

4. **Preheat and Shape:** Preheat oven to 350°F (175°C). Roll out the dough on a floured surface to about 1/4-inch thickness. Cut into shapes with cookie cutters.

5. **Bake:** Place cookies on a lined baking sheet and bake for 8-10 minutes or until edges are lightly browned. Cool before serving.

Nutritional Values (per cookie):

- **Calories:** 90
- **Carbohydrates:** 12g
- **Protein:** 1g
- **Fat:** 4g
- **Fiber:** 1g

Tips & Tricks:

- Decorate with icing or sprinkles for a festive touch.
- For a chewier texture, slightly underbake the cookies.
- Dough can be stored in the fridge for up to 3 days before baking.

Lemon Drizzle Cake

Preparation Time: 15 minutes
Cooking Time: 45 minutes
Servings: 10 slices

Ingredients:

- 1/2 cup sourdough discard
- 1 1/2 cups all-purpose flour
- 1 teaspoon baking powder
- 1/4 teaspoon salt
- 1/2 cup unsalted butter, softened
- 1 cup granulated sugar
- 2 large eggs
- Zest of 2 lemons
- 1/2 cup milk
- **Lemon Drizzle:**
    - 1/4 cup lemon juice
    - 1/2 cup powdered sugar

Directions:

1. **Prepare Batter:** In a medium bowl, mix flour, baking powder, and salt. In another bowl, cream butter and sugar until fluffy. Add eggs, one at a time, followed by lemon zest and sourdough discard.

2. **Combine Ingredients:** Gradually add dry ingredients and milk to the creamed mixture, alternating between the two until a smooth batter forms.

3. **Bake:** Pour the batter into a greased loaf pan. Bake at 350°F (175°C) for 40-45 minutes or until a toothpick comes out clean.
4. **Make Drizzle:** While the cake cools, mix lemon juice and powdered sugar to form the drizzle. Pour over the cooled cake.

Nutritional Values (per serving):
- **Calories:** 180
- **Carbohydrates:** 27g
- **Protein:** 3g
- **Fat:** 7g
- **Fiber:** 1g

Tips & Tricks:
- For an intense lemon flavor, add lemon zest to the drizzle.
- Use a skewer to poke small holes in the cake before drizzling for better absorption.
- Store at room temperature for up to 3 days.

Sourdough Carrot Cake

Preparation Time: 20 minutes
Cooking Time: 35 minutes
Servings: 12 slices

Ingredients:
- 1/2 cup sourdough discard
- 1 1/2 cups all-purpose flour
- 1/2 cup granulated sugar
- 1/2 cup brown sugar, packed
- 1 teaspoon baking powder
- 1/2 teaspoon baking soda
- 1 teaspoon cinnamon
- 1/4 teaspoon nutmeg
- 1/4 teaspoon salt
- 1/2 cup vegetable oil
- 2 large eggs
- 1 1/2 cups grated carrots
- 1/2 cup chopped walnuts (optional)
- **Cream Cheese Frosting:**
    - 1/2 cup cream cheese, softened
    - 1/4 cup unsalted butter, softened
    - 1 cup powdered sugar
    - 1 teaspoon vanilla extract

Directions:
1. **Prepare Batter:** In a large bowl, combine flour, sugars, baking powder, baking soda, cinnamon, nutmeg, and salt. In a separate bowl, mix oil, eggs, and sourdough discard until smooth.
2. **Combine Ingredients:** Add wet ingredients to dry, stirring until combined. Fold in grated carrots and walnuts if using.
3. **Bake:** Pour the batter into a greased 9-inch cake pan. Bake at 350°F (175°C) for 30-35 minutes or until a toothpick comes out clean.
4. **Prepare Frosting:** Beat cream cheese and butter until smooth. Gradually add powdered sugar and vanilla.

5. **Frost Cake:** Let the cake cool before spreading the cream cheese frosting on top.

Nutritional Values (per serving):

- **Calories:** 290
- **Carbohydrates:** 36g
- **Protein:** 4g
- **Fat:** 14g
- **Fiber:** 2g

Tips & Tricks:

- For extra flavor, add a pinch of ground ginger.
- This cake stays moist when stored in the refrigerator for up to 5 days.
- Decorate with extra chopped walnuts on top of the frosting for added texture.

Coconut Macaroons

Preparation Time: 10 minutes
Cooking Time: 20 minutes
Servings: 20 macaroons

Ingredients:

- 1/2 cup sourdough discard
- 2 1/2 cups shredded unsweetened coconut
- 1/2 cup granulated sugar
- 2 large egg whites
- 1 teaspoon vanilla extract
- 1/4 teaspoon salt
- Optional: 1/2 cup chocolate chips for dipping

Directions:

1. **Prepare Mixture:** In a large bowl, combine the sourdough discard, shredded coconut, sugar, egg whites, vanilla extract, and salt. Stir until fully combined.
2. **Shape Macaroons:** Using a tablespoon, scoop the mixture and shape it into small mounds. Place each mound on a baking sheet lined with parchment paper.
3. **Bake:** Preheat oven to 325°F (165°C) and bake for 18-20 minutes, or until the edges are golden.
4. **Cool and Dip (Optional):** Let the macaroons cool, then dip the bottoms in melted chocolate if desired. Place on parchment paper to set.

Nutritional Values (per serving):

- **Calories:** 80
- **Carbohydrates:** 10g
- **Protein:** 1g
- **Fat:** 4g
- **Fiber:** 1g

Tips & Tricks:

- For a tropical twist, add a pinch of lime zest.
- Store macaroons in an airtight container at room temperature for up to a week.
- Ensure the mixture is moist enough to stick together before shaping.

Sticky Toffee Pudding

Preparation Time: 15 minutes
Cooking Time: 40 minutes
Servings: 8 servings

Ingredients:

- 1/2 cup sourdough discard
- 1 cup all-purpose flour
- 1 teaspoon baking powder
- 1/4 teaspoon salt
- 1/2 cup chopped dates
- 1/4 cup boiling water
- 1/4 cup brown sugar
- 1/4 cup unsalted butter, softened
- 2 large eggs
- **Toffee Sauce:**
    - 1/2 cup brown sugar
    - 1/4 cup heavy cream
    - 1/4 cup unsalted butter

Directions:

1. **Prepare Dates:** Soak chopped dates in boiling water for 5 minutes until softened, then mash.
2. **Mix Batter:** In a bowl, cream butter and brown sugar until fluffy. Add eggs and sourdough discard, mixing until smooth. Add flour, baking powder, and salt, then stir in the mashed dates.
3. **Bake:** Pour batter into a greased baking dish and bake at 350°F (175°C) for 35-40 minutes.
4. **Make Toffee Sauce:** In a saucepan, combine brown sugar, cream, and butter over medium heat. Stir until smooth and simmer for 3 minutes.
5. **Serve:** Pour warm toffee sauce over pudding and serve immediately.

Nutritional Values (per serving):

- **Calories:** 320
- **Carbohydrates:** 42g
- **Protein:** 3g
- **Fat:** 16g
- **Fiber:** 2g

Tips & Tricks:

- For a richer sauce, add a splash of vanilla extract to the toffee.
- Sticky toffee pudding is best enjoyed warm; reheat leftovers in the microwave.

Chocolate Chip Cookies

Preparation Time: 10 minutes
Cooking Time: 12 minutes
Servings: 24 cookies

Ingredients:

- 1/2 cup sourdough discard
- 1 cup all-purpose flour
- 1/2 teaspoon baking soda
- 1/4 teaspoon salt
- 1/2 cup unsalted butter, softened
- 1/2 cup brown sugar, packed
- 1/4 cup granulated sugar

- 1 large egg
- 1 teaspoon vanilla extract
- 1 cup chocolate chips

Directions:

1. **Mix Dough:** Cream together the butter, brown sugar, and granulated sugar until fluffy. Add the egg, vanilla, and sourdough discard, mixing until smooth.

2. **Combine Dry Ingredients:** In a separate bowl, whisk flour, baking soda, and salt. Gradually add dry ingredients to the wet mixture, stirring until just combined. Fold in chocolate chips.

3. **Bake:** Drop rounded tablespoons of dough onto a lined baking sheet. Bake at 350°F (175°C) for 10-12 minutes or until golden brown on the edges.

Nutritional Values (per cookie):

- **Calories:** 100
- **Carbohydrates:** 14g
- **Protein:** 1g
- **Fat:** 5g
- **Fiber:** 1g

Tips & Tricks:

- For chewy cookies, slightly underbake by 1-2 minutes.
- Use a combination of milk and dark chocolate chips for extra flavor.
- Dough can be frozen for up to 3 months; bake directly from frozen.

Double Chocolate Cake

Preparation Time: 20 minutes
Cooking Time: 30 minutes
Servings: 12 slices

Ingredients:

- 1/2 cup sourdough discard
- 1 1/2 cups all-purpose flour
- 1/2 cup unsweetened cocoa powder
- 1 teaspoon baking soda
- 1/2 teaspoon salt
- 1/2 cup unsalted butter, melted
- 1 cup granulated sugar
- 2 large eggs
- 1 teaspoon vanilla extract
- 1 cup buttermilk
- **Chocolate Frosting:**
    - 1/2 cup unsalted butter, softened
    - 1/4 cup cocoa powder
    - 2 cups powdered sugar
    - 1-2 tablespoons milk

Directions:

1. **Prepare Batter:** In a bowl, combine flour, cocoa powder, baking soda, and salt. In another bowl, mix melted butter, sugar, eggs, vanilla, sourdough discard, and buttermilk until smooth.

2. **Combine and Bake:** Gradually add dry ingredients to the wet mixture. Pour batter into a greased 9-inch

round pan and bake at 350°F (175°C) for 30-35 minutes.

3. **Make Frosting:** Cream butter and cocoa powder. Gradually add powdered sugar and milk, beating until smooth.

4. **Frost and Serve:** Let cake cool before frosting.

Nutritional Values (per serving):

- **Calories:** 280
- **Carbohydrates:** 36g
- **Protein:** 4g
- **Fat:** 13g
- **Fiber:** 2g

Tips & Tricks:

- For richer flavor, add a teaspoon of espresso powder.
- Garnish with chocolate shavings for a finishing touch.
- Store cake in the refrigerator to maintain freshness.

Blueberry Buckle

Preparation Time: 15 minutes
Cooking Time: 40 minutes
Servings: 9 slices

Ingredients:

- 1/2 cup sourdough discard
- 1 cup all-purpose flour
- 1/2 cup granulated sugar
- 1 teaspoon baking powder
- 1/4 teaspoon salt
- 1/2 cup unsalted butter, softened
- 1 large egg
- 1/4 cup milk
- 1 cup fresh blueberries
- Topping:
  - 1/4 cup flour
  - 1/4 cup brown sugar
  - 2 tablespoons butter, melted

Directions:

1. **Prepare Batter:** Cream butter and sugar until fluffy. Add egg, sourdough discard, and milk, mixing until smooth. In another bowl, combine flour, baking powder, and salt, then add to the wet mixture.

2. **Add Blueberries:** Gently fold in blueberries and spread batter in a greased 9-inch pan.

3. **Make Topping and Bake:** Combine topping ingredients and sprinkle over batter. Bake at 350°F (175°C) for 35-40 minutes.

Nutritional Values (per serving):

- **Calories:** 210
- **Carbohydrates:** 28g
- **Protein:** 3g
- **Fat:** 10g
- **Fiber:** 1g

Tips & Tricks:

- Use frozen blueberries if fresh are not available, but do not thaw them before adding.

- Serve with a scoop of vanilla ice cream for a delightful treat.
- Store leftovers in an airtight container for up to 3 days.

Raspberry Bars

Preparation Time: 15 minutes
Cooking Time: 35 minutes
Servings: 12 bars

Ingredients:

- 1/2 cup sourdough discard
- 1 1/2 cups all-purpose flour
- 1/2 cup granulated sugar
- 1/2 teaspoon baking powder
- 1/4 teaspoon salt
- 3/4 cup unsalted butter, cold and cubed
- 1 cup raspberry jam
- 1/2 cup shredded coconut (optional)

Directions:

1. **Prepare Crust:** In a bowl, combine flour, sugar, baking powder, and salt. Cut in cold butter until the mixture resembles coarse crumbs. Reserve 1/2 cup for the topping.
2. **Add Sourdough and Assemble:** Mix in sourdough discard until a dough forms. Press into the bottom of a greased 9x9-inch pan. Spread raspberry jam evenly over the dough.
3. **Add Topping and Bake:** Sprinkle the reserved crumbs and shredded coconut over the jam. Bake at 350°F (175°C) for 30-35 minutes or until golden.

Nutritional Values (per serving):

- **Calories:** 210
- **Carbohydrates:** 29g
- **Protein:** 2g
- **Fat:** 10g
- **Fiber:** 1g

Tips & Tricks:

- For extra texture, add chopped nuts to the topping.
- Swap raspberry jam with strawberry or apricot for variety.
- Allow bars to cool fully before slicing for clean cuts.

Biscotti with Almonds

Preparation Time: 20 minutes
Cooking Time: 45 minutes
Servings: 18 biscotti

Ingredients:

- 1/2 cup sourdough discard
- 1 3/4 cups all-purpose flour
- 3/4 cup granulated sugar
- 1 teaspoon baking powder
- 1/4 teaspoon salt
- 1/2 teaspoon almond extract
- 1/4 cup unsalted butter, softened
- 2 large eggs
- 1/2 cup sliced almonds

Directions:

1. **Prepare Dough:** In a large bowl, combine flour, sugar, baking powder,

and salt. In another bowl, beat together butter, eggs, sourdough discard, and almond extract until smooth. Add dry ingredients and fold in almonds.

2. **Shape and Bake:** Divide dough in half and shape into two 10-inch logs on a lined baking sheet. Bake at 350°F (175°C) for 25 minutes, then cool for 10 minutes.

3. **Slice and Re-Bake:** Slice each log into 1/2-inch pieces. Arrange slices on the baking sheet and bake for an additional 15-20 minutes, flipping halfway.

Nutritional Values (per biscotti):

- **Calories:** 110
- **Carbohydrates:** 14g
- **Protein:** 3g
- **Fat:** 5g
- **Fiber:** 1g

Tips & Tricks:

- For a chocolate variation, dip one end of each biscotti in melted chocolate.
- Store biscotti in an airtight container for up to two weeks.
- Adjust baking time for softer or crunchier biscotti.

Donuts with Sourdough Base

Preparation Time: 20 minutes (plus 1 hour rising)
Cooking Time: 10 minutes
Servings: 12 donuts

Ingredients:

- 1/2 cup sourdough discard
- 2 cups all-purpose flour
- 1/4 cup granulated sugar
- 1/2 teaspoon salt
- 1/2 cup milk, warmed
- 1/4 cup unsalted butter, melted
- 1 large egg
- Vegetable oil, for frying
- **Glaze (optional):**
  - 1 cup powdered sugar
  - 2-3 tablespoons milk
  - 1/2 teaspoon vanilla extract

Directions:

1. **Prepare Dough:** In a bowl, mix flour, sugar, and salt. Add sourdough discard, warm milk, melted butter, and egg, kneading until smooth. Cover and let rise for 1 hour.

2. **Shape Donuts:** Roll out the dough to 1/2-inch thickness. Use a donut cutter to cut out shapes. Let rest for 10 minutes.

3. **Fry Donuts:** Heat oil to 350°F (175°C) in a deep pan. Fry donuts for 1-2 minutes per side until golden. Drain on paper towels.

4. **Glaze (Optional):** Whisk powdered sugar, milk, and vanilla extract until smooth. Dip donuts in glaze if desired.

Nutritional Values (per donut):

- **Calories:** 190
- **Carbohydrates:** 25g

- **Protein:** 3g
- **Fat:** 8g
- **Fiber:** 1g

Tips & Tricks:

- For a cinnamon-sugar coating, roll hot donuts in a mixture of sugar and cinnamon.
- For baked donuts, bake at 350°F (175°C) for 12-15 minutes instead of frying.
- Leftover donuts can be reheated in an air fryer for a fresh taste.

Boston Cream Pie

Preparation Time: 30 minutes
Cooking Time: 25 minutes
Chilling Time: 1 hour
Servings: 10 slices

Ingredients:

- **Cake:**
    - 1/2 cup sourdough discard
    - 1 1/2 cups all-purpose flour
    - 1 teaspoon baking powder
    - 1/4 teaspoon salt
    - 1/2 cup unsalted butter, softened
    - 1 cup granulated sugar
    - 2 large eggs
    - 1/2 cup milk
- **Filling:**
    - 1 cup milk
    - 1/4 cup granulated sugar
    - 2 tablespoons cornstarch
    - 2 large egg yolks
    - 1/2 teaspoon vanilla extract
- **Chocolate Ganache:**
    - 1/2 cup heavy cream
    - 1/2 cup chocolate chips

Directions:

1. **Prepare Cake Layers:** Cream butter and sugar until fluffy. Add eggs, one at a time, and sourdough discard. Gradually add flour, baking powder, salt, and milk. Divide into two greased 9-inch pans and bake at 350°F (175°C) for 20-25 minutes.
2. **Make Filling:** In a saucepan, heat milk. In another bowl, whisk sugar, cornstarch, and egg yolks, then add to hot milk, stirring until thickened. Add vanilla and chill.
3. **Assemble and Add Ganache:** Spread filling between cake layers. Heat cream, pour over chocolate chips, and stir until smooth. Spread ganache over the top layer.

Nutritional Values (per slice):

- **Calories:** 310
- **Carbohydrates:** 39g
- **Protein:** 5g
- **Fat:** 14g
- **Fiber:** 1g

Tips & Tricks:

- Chill cake thoroughly for the filling to set.

- Use dark chocolate for a less sweet ganache.
- Store leftovers in the refrigerator for up to 3 days.

Apple Pie with Sourdough Crust

Preparation Time: 40 minutes
Cooking Time: 50 minutes
Servings: 8 slices

Ingredients:

- **Crust:**
    - 1/2 cup sourdough discard
    - 2 cups all-purpose flour
    - 1/2 teaspoon salt
    - 1/2 cup cold unsalted butter, cubed
    - 3-4 tablespoons ice water
- **Filling:**
    - 6 cups sliced apples (Granny Smith or Honeycrisp)
    - 3/4 cup granulated sugar
    - 1/4 cup brown sugar
    - 1 teaspoon cinnamon
    - 1/4 teaspoon nutmeg
    - 2 tablespoons flour

Directions:

1. **Prepare Crust:** In a bowl, combine flour and salt. Cut in butter until mixture resembles coarse crumbs. Mix in sourdough discard and ice water until dough forms. Divide in half, roll out, and line a 9-inch pie plate with one half.
2. **Make Filling:** Toss apples with sugars, cinnamon, nutmeg, and flour. Fill pie crust with apple mixture.
3. **Assemble and Bake:** Roll out remaining dough, place over filling, and crimp edges. Cut slits in the top crust and bake at 375°F (190°C) for 50-55 minutes.

Nutritional Values (per slice):

- **Calories:** 320
- **Carbohydrates:** 55g
- **Protein:** 3g
- **Fat:** 12g
- **Fiber:** 4g

Tips & Tricks:

- Brush the top crust with egg wash for a golden finish.
- For a sweeter filling, mix in a tablespoon of honey.
- Let pie cool for at least an hour before slicing.

Pumpkin Pie with Sourdough Crust

Preparation Time: 30 minutes
Cooking Time: 1 hour
Servings: 8 slices

Ingredients:

- **Crust:**
    - 1/2 cup sourdough discard
    - 2 cups all-purpose flour
    - 1/2 teaspoon salt

- o 1/2 cup cold unsalted butter, cubed
- o 3-4 tablespoons ice water
- **Filling:**
  - o 1 can (15 ounces) pumpkin puree
  - o 3/4 cup brown sugar
  - o 1 teaspoon ground cinnamon
  - o 1/2 teaspoon ground ginger
  - o 1/4 teaspoon ground cloves
  - o 1/4 teaspoon salt
  - o 2 large eggs
  - o 1 cup evaporated milk

Directions:

1. **Prepare Crust:** Combine flour and salt in a bowl. Cut in butter until mixture resembles coarse crumbs. Add sourdough discard and ice water until dough forms. Roll out and press into a 9-inch pie plate.

2. **Make Filling:** In a bowl, mix pumpkin puree, brown sugar, cinnamon, ginger, cloves, salt, eggs, and evaporated milk until smooth.

3. **Bake:** Pour filling into crust and bake at 350°F (175°C) for 50-60 minutes or until the center is set.

Nutritional Values (per slice):

- **Calories:** 280
- **Carbohydrates:** 40g
- **Protein:** 4g
- **Fat:** 12g
- **Fiber:** 3g

Tips & Tricks:

- For an extra spiced flavor, add a pinch of nutmeg.
- Use fresh pumpkin puree for a homemade touch.
- Cool pie completely before slicing for the best texture.

Tiramisu with Sourdough Ladyfingers

Preparation Time: 30 minutes (plus 4 hours chilling)
Servings: 9 squares

Ingredients:

- **Ladyfingers:**
  - o 1/2 cup sourdough discard
  - o 1 cup all-purpose flour
  - o 1/4 teaspoon baking powder
  - o 3 large eggs, separated
  - o 1/2 cup granulated sugar
- **Filling:**
  - o 1 cup mascarpone cheese
  - o 1/2 cup heavy cream
  - o 1/4 cup powdered sugar
  - o 1 cup brewed coffee, cooled
  - o 2 tablespoons cocoa powder

Directions:

1. **Make Ladyfingers:** Preheat oven to 350°F (175°C). Whip egg yolks and half the sugar until pale. In a separate bowl, whisk egg whites and remaining sugar to stiff peaks. Fold in sourdough discard, flour, and

baking powder. Pipe into ladyfinger shapes on a baking sheet and bake for 10-12 minutes.

2. **Prepare Filling:** Whisk mascarpone, heavy cream, and powdered sugar until smooth.

3. **Assemble Tiramisu:** Dip ladyfingers in coffee and layer in an 8x8 dish. Spread mascarpone mixture on top, repeat layers, and dust with cocoa powder. Chill for 4 hours.

Nutritional Values (per serving):

- **Calories:** 310
- **Carbohydrates:** 32g
- **Protein:** 6g
- **Fat:** 18g
- **Fiber:** 1g

Tips & Tricks:

- For a richer flavor, add a splash of coffee liqueur.
- Make this dessert a day ahead to let the flavors meld.
- Dust with extra cocoa before serving for presentation.

Chocolate Truffles

Preparation Time: 15 minutes (plus 2 hours chilling)
Servings: 24 truffles

Ingredients:

- 1/2 cup sourdough discard
- 1 cup dark chocolate chips
- 1/2 cup heavy cream
- 1/4 teaspoon vanilla extract
- Cocoa powder or powdered sugar, for rolling

Directions:

1. **Melt Chocolate:** In a heatproof bowl, melt chocolate chips with heavy cream until smooth. Stir in sourdough discard and vanilla.

2. **Chill Mixture:** Refrigerate for 2 hours or until firm enough to roll.

3. **Shape Truffles:** Use a spoon to scoop out small portions, roll into balls, and coat with cocoa powder or powdered sugar.

Nutritional Values (per truffle):

- **Calories:** 60
- **Carbohydrates:** 5g
- **Protein:** 1g
- **Fat:** 4g
- **Fiber:** 1g

Tips & Tricks:

- For a flavor variation, add a pinch of sea salt.
- Truffles can be stored in the fridge for up to a week.
- Try rolling in shredded coconut for an extra layer of texture.

Lemon Bars

Preparation Time: 15 minutes
Cooking Time: 40 minutes
Servings: 16 bars

Ingredients:

- **Crust:**
    - 1/2 cup sourdough discard
    - 1 cup all-purpose flour
    - 1/4 cup granulated sugar
    - 1/2 cup cold unsalted butter, cubed
- **Filling:**
    - 1 cup granulated sugar
    - 1/4 cup all-purpose flour
    - 3 large eggs
    - 1/2 cup lemon juice
    - Zest of 1 lemon

Directions:

1. **Prepare Crust:** Combine flour, sugar, and butter, cutting in butter until it resembles coarse crumbs. Mix in sourdough discard, then press into an 8x8-inch pan. Bake at 350°F (175°C) for 15 minutes.
2. **Make Filling:** Whisk sugar, flour, eggs, lemon juice, and zest until smooth. Pour over the crust.
3. **Bake:** Return to the oven for 25 minutes or until set.

Nutritional Values (per bar):

- **Calories:** 140
- **Carbohydrates:** 20g
- **Protein:** 2g
- **Fat:** 6g
- **Fiber:** 1g

Tips & Tricks:

- Dust with powdered sugar for a classic look.
- Add more lemon zest for a stronger lemon flavor.
- Chill before slicing for cleaner cuts.

Peach Cobbler

Preparation Time: 10 minutes
Cooking Time: 35 minutes
Servings: 8 slices

Ingredients:

- 1/2 cup sourdough discard
- 1 cup all-purpose flour
- 1/2 cup granulated sugar
- 1 teaspoon baking powder
- 1/2 teaspoon salt
- 1/2 cup milk
- 1/4 cup unsalted butter, melted
- 4 cups sliced peaches
- 1/4 cup brown sugar
- 1/2 teaspoon cinnamon

Directions:

1. **Prepare Batter:** Combine flour, sugar, baking powder, and salt. Stir in milk, melted butter, and sourdough discard until smooth.
2. **Assemble Cobbler:** Pour batter into a greased 9x9-inch pan, then layer sliced peaches over the top. Sprinkle with brown sugar and cinnamon.
3. **Bake:** Bake at 350°F (175°C) for 35 minutes, or until golden brown.

Nutritional Values (per slice):

- **Calories:** 180
- **Carbohydrates:** 30g
- **Protein:** 2g
- **Fat:** 6g
- **Fiber:** 2g

Tips & Tricks:

- Substitute with other seasonal fruits like apples or berries.
- Serve warm with a scoop of vanilla ice cream.
- To avoid a soggy bottom, slightly pre-cook the peaches.

Mug Cake

Preparation Time: 5 minutes
Cooking Time: 1 minute
Servings: 1 serving

Ingredients:

- 2 tablespoons sourdough discard
- 2 tablespoons all-purpose flour
- 2 tablespoons granulated sugar
- 1 tablespoon cocoa powder
- 1/4 teaspoon baking powder
- 2 tablespoons milk
- 1 tablespoon vegetable oil
- 1/4 teaspoon vanilla extract

Directions:

1. **Mix Ingredients:** In a microwave-safe mug, combine flour, sugar, cocoa powder, baking powder, milk, oil, vanilla extract, and sourdough discard.
2. **Microwave:** Microwave on high for 1 minute or until set.

Nutritional Values (per serving):

- **Calories:** 210
- **Carbohydrates:** 30g
- **Protein:** 2g
- **Fat:** 10g
- **Fiber:** 1g

Tips & Tricks:

- Add chocolate chips for a gooey center.
- Top with a scoop of ice cream for an extra treat.
- Adjust microwave time based on wattage; start with 30-second increments.

Cherry Clafoutis

Preparation Time: 15 minutes
Cooking Time: 35 minutes
Servings: 6 servings

Ingredients:

- 1/2 cup sourdough discard
- 1/2 cup all-purpose flour
- 1/4 cup granulated sugar
- 1 cup milk
- 3 large eggs
- 1/2 teaspoon vanilla extract
- 2 cups pitted cherries

Directions:

1. **Prepare Batter:** In a large bowl, whisk together the sourdough discard, flour, and sugar until well combined. Add the milk, eggs, and vanilla extract, and continue whisking until the batter is smooth and free of lumps.
2. **Arrange Cherries:** Grease a 9-inch pie dish or baking dish, then arrange the pitted cherries evenly across the bottom of the dish.
3. **Pour Batter and Bake:** Pour the batter over the cherries, covering them completely. Bake at 350°F (175°C) for 35-40 minutes, or until the clafoutis is puffed up and golden brown around the edges.
4. **Cool and Serve:** Allow the clafoutis to cool slightly before serving. It can be enjoyed warm or at room temperature.

Nutritional Values (per serving):

- **Calories:** 180
- **Carbohydrates:** 27g
- **Protein:** 6g
- **Fat:** 5g
- **Fiber:** 2g

Tips & Tricks:

- For a twist, sprinkle a light dusting of powdered sugar on top before serving.
- Substitute cherries with other fruits like blueberries or sliced peaches for different flavors.
- Clafoutis can be stored in the refrigerator for up to 2 days and reheated gently.

Sweet Biscuit Shortcake

Preparation Time: 20 minutes
Cooking Time: 15 minutes
Servings: 8 shortcakes

Ingredients:

- 1/2 cup sourdough discard
- 1 1/2 cups all-purpose flour
- 1/4 cup granulated sugar
- 1 tablespoon baking powder
- 1/4 teaspoon salt
- 1/2 cup cold unsalted butter, cubed
- 1/2 cup milk
- **For Serving:**
    - Fresh strawberries or other berries
    - Whipped cream

Directions:

1. **Prepare Dough:** In a large bowl, mix the flour, sugar, baking powder, and salt. Cut in the cold butter until the mixture resembles coarse crumbs. Stir in the sourdough discard and milk until just combined.
2. **Shape and Bake:** Turn the dough out onto a lightly floured surface and pat it into a 1-inch thick round. Use a biscuit cutter to cut out shortcakes, then place them on a lined baking sheet. Bake at 400°F (200°C) for 12-15 minutes, or until golden brown.
3. **Serve:** Slice each shortcake in half and layer with fresh berries and whipped cream.

Nutritional Values (per serving):

- **Calories:** 220
- **Carbohydrates:** 30g
- **Protein:** 4g
- **Fat:** 10g
- **Fiber:** 1g

Tips & Tricks:

- Add a hint of vanilla extract to the whipped cream for extra flavor.
- Substitute berries with other seasonal fruits for variety.
- Shortcakes are best served fresh but can be stored in an airtight container for up to 2 days.

CHAPTER 6: VERSATILE DOUGHS & BATTERS

All-Purpose Discard Dough

This multipurpose dough works well in a variety of savory and sweet applications, making it an ideal go-to option for busy days. The sourdough discard adds a subtle tang, enhancing flavor while reducing waste.

- **Preparation Time:** 10 minutes
- **Resting Time:** 1 hour
- **Servings:** 4

Ingredients

- 1 cup sourdough discard
- 2 cups all-purpose flour
- 1/2 cup water
- 1 tsp salt
- 1 tsp sugar
- 1/4 cup olive oil

Directions

1. In a large mixing bowl, combine the sourdough discard, flour, and water. Mix until the dough comes together.
2. Add salt, sugar, and olive oil, kneading for 5-7 minutes until smooth.
3. Cover with a damp cloth and let rest for 1 hour before using.
4. Roll or shape as desired for pizzas, flatbreads, or breadsticks.

Nutritional Values *(per serving)*

- Calories: 150
- Protein: 4g
- Carbohydrates: 28g
- Fat: 5g

Tips & Tricks

- Substitute whole wheat flour for a denser texture.
- To freeze, portion dough and store in airtight bags.

Basic Bread Dough

A classic and reliable dough, this recipe is perfect for creating soft, flavorful loaves with minimal effort. The sourdough discard provides natural leavening, simplifying the bread-making process.

- **Preparation Time:** 15 minutes
- **Cooking Time:** 30 minutes
- **Servings:** 1 loaf

Ingredients

- 1 cup sourdough discard
- 3 cups bread flour
- 1 1/2 cups warm water
- 1 tbsp sugar
- 1 tsp salt

Directions

1. Mix discard, warm water, and sugar in a bowl until well combined.
2. Gradually add bread flour and salt, kneading until dough is smooth.
3. Let rise in a warm place for 2 hours, then shape into a loaf.
4. Bake at 375°F for 30 minutes until golden brown.

Nutritional Values *(per slice)*

- Calories: 120

- Protein: 3g
- Carbohydrates: 22g
- Fat: 1g

Tips & Tricks
- Score the dough for a rustic appearance.
- Brush with olive oil before baking for a golden crust.

Empanada Dough

Perfect for savory or sweet fillings, this empanada dough adds a tangy flavor that complements a variety of ingredients, making it an ideal option for family gatherings or meal prep.

- **Preparation Time:** 20 minutes
- **Resting Time:** 1 hour
- **Servings:** 12 empanadas

Ingredients
- 1 cup sourdough discard
- 2 cups flour
- 1/2 cup butter, chilled and diced
- 1/4 cup water
- 1/2 tsp salt

Directions
1. Combine flour, salt, and butter in a food processor until crumbly.
2. Add sourdough discard and water, mixing until dough forms.
3. Wrap in plastic and refrigerate for 1 hour before rolling.
4. Roll dough into circles, fill as desired, and bake at 350°F for 20 minutes.

Nutritional Values *(per empanada)*
- Calories: 100
- Protein: 2g
- Carbohydrates: 15g
- Fat: 3g

Tips & Tricks
- For crispier empanadas, brush with egg wash before baking.
- Store leftover dough in the fridge for up to 3 days.

Soft Pizza Dough

This dough creates a light and airy crust with just the right amount of chewiness, making it perfect for pizzas loaded with family-favorite toppings.

- **Preparation Time:** 15 minutes
- **Resting Time:** 1 hour
- **Servings:** 2 large pizzas

Ingredients
- 1 cup sourdough discard
- 3 cups all-purpose flour
- 1 cup warm water
- 1 tsp salt
- 1 tbsp olive oil

Directions
1. Combine discard and warm water in a large bowl. Add flour and salt, mixing until smooth.

2. Knead for 10 minutes and let rise for 1 hour.
3. Divide into two balls, roll out, and top with favorite ingredients.
4. Bake at 450°F for 10-12 minutes.

Nutritional Values *(per slice)*

- Calories: 80
- Protein: 3g
- Carbohydrates: 14g
- Fat: 2g

Tips & Tricks

- For a crispier crust, bake on a pizza stone.
- Pre-bake crust for 5 minutes before adding toppings.

Pastry Dough for Pies

This dough yields a flaky, golden crust ideal for both sweet and savory pies. The sourdough discard adds depth of flavor and pairs wonderfully with all types of fillings.

- **Preparation Time:** 20 minutes
- **Resting Time:** 30 minutes
- **Servings:** 1 pie crust

Ingredients

- 1 cup sourdough discard
- 2 cups pastry flour
- 1/2 cup butter, cold and cubed
- 1/4 cup ice water
- 1 tsp salt

Directions

1. Mix flour and salt, then cut in butter until mixture resembles coarse crumbs.
2. Add sourdough discard and ice water, forming a dough.
3. Wrap in plastic and refrigerate for 30 minutes.
4. Roll out, fill, and bake as desired.

Nutritional Values *(per slice)*

- Calories: 200
- Protein: 2g
- Carbohydrates: 18g
- Fat: 14g

Tips & Tricks

- Avoid overworking the dough for flakier results.
- Chill the dough before rolling for easier handling.

Crepe Batter

This light and versatile batter produces delicate crepes that can be filled with an endless variety of ingredients, perfect for breakfast or dessert.

- **Preparation Time:** 10 minutes
- **Resting Time:** 30 minutes
- **Servings:** 10 crepes

Ingredients

- 1 cup sourdough discard
- 1 cup milk
- 1 cup flour
- 2 eggs

- 1 tbsp sugar

Directions

1. Whisk eggs and sugar, then add sourdough discard and milk.
2. Gradually add flour until smooth.
3. Rest for 30 minutes, then cook in a non-stick pan until golden.

Nutritional Values *(per crepe)*

- Calories: 80
- Protein: 3g
- Carbohydrates: 11g
- Fat: 3g

Tips & Tricks

- Use a thin layer of batter for delicate crepes.
- Keep the pan hot for evenly cooked crepes.

Pancake Batter with Sourdough

These pancakes are fluffy with a mild tang, making them a delicious breakfast staple.

- **Preparation Time:** 10 minutes
- **Cooking Time:** 10 minutes
- **Servings:** 4

Ingredients

- 1 cup sourdough discard
- 1 cup flour
- 1 cup milk
- 1 egg
- 1 tsp baking powder

Directions

1. Whisk egg, milk, and discard together.
2. Add flour and baking powder, mixing until smooth.
3. Cook in a skillet over medium heat until bubbles form, then flip and cook through.

Nutritional Values *(per pancake)*

- Calories: 60
- Protein: 2g
- Carbohydrates: 10g
- Fat: 2g

Tips & Tricks

- Use fresh baking powder for fluffier pancakes.
- Customize with mix-ins like berries or chocolate chips.

CHAPTER 7: DECADENT DELIGHTS & GOURMET BITES

Cranberry Orange Scones

Preparation Time: 15 minutes
Cooking Time: 20 minutes
Servings: 8 scones

Ingredients

- **2 cups** all-purpose flour
- **1/4 cup** granulated sugar
- **1 tbsp** baking powder
- **1/2 tsp** salt
- **1/2 cup** cold, unsalted butter (cubed)
- **1/2 cup** dried cranberries
- **1 tbsp** orange zest
- **1/2 cup** sourdough discard (unfed)
- **1/3 cup** heavy cream (plus extra for brushing)
- **1 large** egg
- **1 tsp** vanilla extract

Directions

1. **Preheat the Oven**: Preheat your oven to 400°F (200°C) and line a baking sheet with parchment paper to prevent sticking.
2. **Prepare the Dry Ingredients**: In a large mixing bowl, combine the flour, sugar, baking powder, and salt. Whisk them together to ensure even distribution of the baking powder.
3. **Incorporate the Butter**: Add the cold, cubed butter into the flour mixture. Using a pastry cutter or your fingers, cut the butter into the flour until the mixture resembles coarse crumbs.
4. **Add the Flavorings**: Stir in the dried cranberries and orange zest. These add a tart sweetness and vibrant aroma that balance beautifully with the sourdough discard.
5. **Combine Wet Ingredients**: In a separate bowl, whisk together the sourdough discard, heavy cream, egg, and vanilla extract until smooth.
6. **Form the Dough**: Pour the wet ingredients into the dry mixture, and gently fold them together. The dough will be slightly sticky, so be careful not to over-mix, which can toughen the scones.
7. **Shape the Scones**: Transfer the dough onto a lightly floured surface and gently shape it into an 8-inch circle. Cut the dough into 8 wedges and place them on the prepared baking sheet, spaced slightly apart.
8. **Brush and Bake**: Lightly brush the tops of the scones with a bit of heavy cream. This helps them develop a golden-brown crust. Bake in the preheated oven for 18-20 minutes or until the scones are golden and a toothpick inserted into the center comes out clean.
9. **Cool and Serve**: Allow the scones to cool slightly on the baking sheet before transferring them to a wire rack. Serve warm for the best texture.

Nutritional Values (per serving)

- **Calories**: 290
- **Total Fat**: 13g
- **Saturated Fat**: 8g

- **Cholesterol**: 50mg
- **Sodium**: 220mg
- **Total Carbohydrate**: 36g
- **Dietary Fiber**: 2g
- **Sugars**: 10g
- **Protein**: 5g

Tips & Tricks

- **Chill Your Ingredients**: Cold butter is essential for creating a flaky texture in scones. You can also chill the flour mixture briefly before adding the wet ingredients.
- **Sourdough Flavor**: If you prefer a tangier flavor, allow your sourdough discard to sit out at room temperature for a few hours before using.
- **Add a Glaze**: For a sweet finish, drizzle a simple orange glaze over the cooled scones. Combine 1/2 cup powdered sugar with 1-2 tablespoons of freshly squeezed orange juice until smooth.

Chocolate Truffle Bites

Preparation Time: 10 minutes (plus chilling)
Cooking Time: 10 minutes
Servings: 12 truffles

Ingredients

- **1/2 cup** sourdough discard
- **1 cup** dark chocolate chips
- **1/2 cup** heavy cream
- **1/4 cup** cocoa powder (for rolling)
- **1/2 tsp** vanilla extract
- Pinch of sea salt

Directions

1. **Heat the Cream**: Warm the heavy cream in a saucepan over low heat until just simmering.
2. **Melt the Chocolate**: Pour the warm cream over chocolate chips in a bowl. Let sit for a minute, then stir until smooth.
3. **Add Sourdough and Flavorings**: Mix in sourdough discard, vanilla, and salt. Chill for 2 hours.
4. **Shape and Roll**: Scoop the mixture, shape into balls, and roll in cocoa powder.

Nutritional Values (per truffle)

- **Calories**: 85
- **Total Fat**: 6g
- **Carbs**: 8g
- **Protein**: 1g

Mini Sourdough Cheesecakes

Preparation Time: 20 minutes
Cooking Time: 20 minutes
Servings: 6 mini cheesecakes

Ingredients

- **1/2 cup** sourdough discard
- **8 oz** cream cheese, softened
- **1/4 cup** sugar
- **1 large egg**
- **1/2 tsp** vanilla extract
- **1/4 cup** graham cracker crumbs (for crust)

Directions

1. **Preheat Oven**: Set to 350°F (175°C). Line a muffin tin with paper liners.
2. **Prepare Crust**: Press a spoonful of graham cracker crumbs into each liner.
3. **Make Cheesecake Mixture**: Blend cream cheese, sugar, sourdough, egg, and vanilla until smooth.
4. **Fill and Bake**: Pour into liners and bake for 20 minutes. Chill before serving.

Nutritional Values (per cheesecake)

- **Calories**: 180
- **Total Fat**: 12g
- **Carbs**: 14g
- **Protein**: 4g

Pumpkin Spice Scones

Preparation Time: 15 minutes
Cooking Time: 18 minutes
Servings: 8 scones

Ingredients

- **2 cups** flour
- **1/4 cup** sugar
- **1 tbsp** baking powder
- **1/2 cup** pumpkin puree
- **1/2 cup** sourdough discard
- **1/2 tsp** pumpkin spice
- **1/4 cup** butter, cubed

Directions

1. **Preheat Oven**: Set to 400°F (200°C).
2. **Combine Ingredients**: Mix dry ingredients, cut in butter, then fold in pumpkin and sourdough.
3. **Shape and Bake**: Form into a circle, cut into 8, bake 18 minutes.

Nutritional Values (per scone)

- **Calories**: 160
- **Total Fat**: 7g
- **Carbs**: 21g
- **Protein**: 3g

Savory Samosas

Preparation Time: 30 minutes
Cooking Time: 20 minutes
Servings: 10 samosas

Ingredients

- **1 cup** sourdough discard
- **1 cup** flour
- **1/4 cup** water
- **2 potatoes**, diced
- **1/2 cup** peas
- **1 tsp** curry powder
- **Salt and pepper**, to taste

Directions

1. **Prepare Dough**: Mix sourdough, flour, and water to make dough.
2. **Cook Filling**: Sauté potatoes, peas, and spices.

3. **Assemble and Fry**: Shape dough, fill with potato mixture, fry until golden.

Nutritional Values (per samosa)

- **Calories**: 90
- **Total Fat**: 3g
- **Carbs**: 14g
- **Protein**: 2g

Blueberry Clafoutis

Preparation Time: 10 minutes
Cooking Time: 30 minutes
Servings: 6

Ingredients

- **1 cup** sourdough discard
- **1 cup** blueberries
- **1/2 cup** sugar
- **1/2 cup** milk
- **3 large eggs**
- **1/2 tsp** vanilla

Directions

1. **Preheat Oven**: Set to 350°F (175°C).
2. **Mix Batter**: Combine sourdough, sugar, milk, eggs, and vanilla.
3. **Add Blueberries**: Pour batter over blueberries in a baking dish. Bake 30 minutes.

Nutritional Values (per serving)

- **Calories**: 160
- **Total Fat**: 5g
- **Carbs**: 22g
- **Protein**: 4g

Tiramisu with Sourdough Layers

Preparation Time: 20 minutes (plus chilling)
Cooking Time: None
Servings: 8

Ingredients

- **1/2 cup** sourdough discard
- **1 cup** mascarpone cheese
- **1 cup** heavy cream
- **1/2 cup** brewed coffee
- **1/2 cup** sugar
- **Cocoa powder** (for dusting)

Directions

1. **Prepare Cream**: Whip mascarpone, sourdough discard, cream, and sugar until smooth.
2. **Layer Tiramisu**: Dip cookies in coffee, layer with mascarpone mixture.
3. **Dust and Chill**: Dust with cocoa powder, refrigerate 4 hours before serving.

Nutritional Values (per serving)

- **Calories**: 220
- **Total Fat**: 14g
- **Carbs**: 18g
- **Protein**: 5g

CHAPTER 8: GUILT-FREE GLUTEN-FREE GOODIES

Gluten-Free Sourdough Pretzels

Preparation Time: 30 minutes
Cooking Time: 20 minutes
Servings: 8 pretzels

Ingredients

- 1 cup gluten-free sourdough discard
- 1 cup warm water
- 1 tbsp sugar
- 2 ¼ tsp active dry yeast
- 1 ½ cups gluten-free all-purpose flour (with xanthan gum)
- ½ cup almond flour
- 1 tbsp melted butter (or olive oil for dairy-free)
- 1 tsp salt
- Coarse sea salt for sprinkling

Directions

1. **Prepare the Yeast Mixture:**
   In a large bowl, combine warm water and sugar, then sprinkle in the active dry yeast. Let it sit for about 5 minutes or until the mixture becomes frothy, which indicates the yeast is activated and ready to use.

2. **Combine with Sourdough Discard:**
   Add the gluten-free sourdough discard to the yeast mixture and stir until smooth. This will incorporate the sourdough flavors while keeping the texture airy and light.

3. **Mix the Flours and Salt:**
   In a separate bowl, whisk together the gluten-free all-purpose flour, almond flour, and salt. This combination ensures that the pretzels remain chewy with a nice texture.

4. **Combine Wet and Dry Ingredients:**
   Gradually add the dry ingredients to the sourdough mixture, mixing until a soft dough forms. If the dough feels too sticky, add a tablespoon of gluten-free flour at a time until it is workable but still soft.

5. **Knead the Dough:**
   On a lightly floured surface, knead the dough for about 5 minutes. Gluten-free dough requires gentle handling, so avoid over-kneading, which can lead to dryness.

6. **Shape the Pretzels:**
   Divide the dough into 8 equal pieces. Roll each piece into a long rope (about 18 inches), then shape it into a classic pretzel form by creating a loop and crossing the ends over each other.

7. **Prepare a Baking Soda Bath:**
   Fill a pot with water and bring it to a gentle boil. Add ¼ cup baking soda. Carefully drop each pretzel into the boiling water for about 15-20 seconds, removing it with a slotted spoon and placing it on a parchment-lined baking sheet.

8. **Brush and Sprinkle:**
   Brush each pretzel with melted butter (or olive oil), then sprinkle with coarse sea salt. This step enhances both the flavor and the traditional appearance of pretzels.

9. **Bake:**
   Preheat the oven to 425°F (220°C).

Bake the pretzels for 15-20 minutes or until they are golden brown. Gluten-free dough tends to brown more quickly, so monitor them closely to avoid burning.

10. **Cool and Serve:**
    Allow the pretzels to cool slightly on a wire rack. Serve warm with your favorite dips, such as mustard or a dairy-free cheese sauce.

Nutritional Values (per pretzel)

- Calories: 170 kcal
- Carbohydrates: 28g
- Protein: 3g
- Fat: 5g
- Fiber: 2g
- Sugar: 1g
- Sodium: 380mg

Tips & Tricks

- **Adjust Flour Mix:** Depending on your gluten-free flour blend, you may need to adjust the amount slightly to get the right consistency. Start with less and add more as needed.

- **Alternative Toppings:** Experiment with toppings like sesame seeds, poppy seeds, or a sprinkling of shredded cheese for variation.

- **Storage Tips:** Store cooled pretzels in an airtight container at room temperature for up to 2 days or freeze for up to a month. Reheat in the oven for the best texture.

Gluten-Free Bagels

Preparation Time: 35 minutes (plus 1 hour for rising)
Cooking Time: 20 minutes
Servings: 6 bagels

Ingredients

- 1 cup gluten-free sourdough discard
- 1 cup warm water
- 1 ½ tsp active dry yeast
- 2 tbsp sugar
- 2 cups gluten-free all-purpose flour (with xanthan gum)
- ¼ cup tapioca starch
- 1 tbsp olive oil
- 1 tsp salt
- 1 tbsp honey (optional, for boiling)
- Toppings: sesame seeds, poppy seeds, or everything bagel seasoning

Directions

1. **Activate the Yeast:**
   In a mixing bowl, combine warm water and sugar, then sprinkle in the active dry yeast. Let sit for 5-10 minutes until it becomes frothy.

2. **Mix with Sourdough Discard:**
   Add the gluten-free sourdough discard to the yeast mixture, stirring until well combined. This enhances flavor and gives the bagels a traditional sourdough tang.

3. **Combine the Flours:**
   In a separate bowl, whisk together the gluten-free all-purpose flour, tapioca starch, and salt. The tapioca

starch helps create the chewy texture essential to bagels.

4. **Form the Dough:**
Gradually add the dry ingredients to the wet mixture, stirring until a dough forms. If the dough is too sticky, add a little more gluten-free flour, one tablespoon at a time, until it holds together but remains soft.

5. **Knead and Rise:**
Lightly knead the dough on a floured surface for about 5 minutes. Place it in a greased bowl, cover, and let rise in a warm area for about 1 hour, or until it has slightly puffed up.

6. **Shape the Bagels:**
Divide the dough into 6 equal portions. Roll each piece into a ball, then poke a hole through the center with your thumb, gently stretching it to form a bagel shape.

7. **Boil the Bagels:**
Bring a pot of water to a gentle boil, and add 1 tbsp of honey for flavor and shine (optional). Boil each bagel for 1 minute on each side, then remove with a slotted spoon and place on a parchment-lined baking sheet.

8. **Add Toppings:**
Brush each bagel with olive oil and sprinkle with desired toppings such as sesame seeds, poppy seeds, or everything bagel seasoning.

9. **Bake:**
Preheat the oven to 425°F (220°C) and bake the bagels for 20-22 minutes or until golden brown. Gluten-free bagels can brown quickly, so keep an eye on them.

10. **Cool and Enjoy:**
Allow bagels to cool on a wire rack before slicing. Enjoy fresh or toasted with your favorite spreads.

Nutritional Values (per bagel)

- Calories: 220 kcal
- Carbohydrates: 36g
- Protein: 4g
- Fat: 5g
- Fiber: 3g
- Sugar: 2g
- Sodium: 400mg

Tips & Tricks

- **Tapioca Starch Alternative:** If you don't have tapioca starch, potato starch can work as a substitute, though the texture may be slightly different.

- **Freezing Instructions:** For long-term storage, freeze cooled bagels in a sealed container. Thaw and toast as needed.

- **Creative Toppings:** Try experimenting with dried onion flakes, garlic powder, or even shredded cheese for a personalized flavor twist.

Gluten-Free Biscuits

Preparation Time: 15 minutes
Cooking Time: 12-15 minutes
Servings: 8 biscuits

Ingredients

- 1 cup gluten-free sourdough discard

- 1 cup gluten-free all-purpose flour (with xanthan gum)
- ¼ cup tapioca starch
- 1 tsp baking powder
- ½ tsp baking soda
- ½ tsp salt
- ¼ cup cold butter or dairy-free alternative (cut into small cubes)
- ¾ cup unsweetened almond milk (or milk of choice)

Directions

1. **Preheat Oven:**
   Preheat your oven to 425°F (220°C). Line a baking sheet with parchment paper to prevent sticking.

2. **Combine Dry Ingredients:**
   In a large bowl, whisk together the gluten-free flour, tapioca starch, baking powder, baking soda, and salt. This mixture helps create a light and fluffy biscuit texture.

3. **Cut in the Butter:**
   Add the cold butter cubes to the flour mixture, using a pastry cutter or your fingers to blend until it resembles coarse crumbs. This step is crucial for a flaky texture, so avoid overworking the butter.

4. **Add Sourdough Discard and Milk:**
   Pour in the gluten-free sourdough discard and almond milk. Gently stir until just combined. The dough should be soft and slightly sticky.

5. **Shape the Biscuits:**
   Turn the dough onto a lightly floured surface. Gently pat it to a 1-inch thickness. Use a biscuit cutter or the rim of a glass to cut out rounds, transferring them to the prepared baking sheet.

6. **Bake:**
   Bake the biscuits in the preheated oven for 12-15 minutes or until golden brown on the top. Gluten-free biscuits can over-bake quickly, so watch carefully in the last few minutes.

7. **Serve Warm:**
   Allow biscuits to cool slightly on a wire rack, then serve warm with butter, jam, or your favorite spreads.

Nutritional Values (per biscuit)

- Calories: 140 kcal
- Carbohydrates: 18g
- Protein: 2g
- Fat: 6g
- Fiber: 1g
- Sugar: 1g
- Sodium: 270mg

Tips & Tricks

- **Dairy-Free Option:** Substitute butter with a plant-based alternative if you prefer a dairy-free version.
- **Storage Tips:** Store cooled biscuits in an airtight container at room temperature for up to 2 days or freeze for up to 1 month.
- **Enhance Flavor:** Add a pinch of garlic powder or dried herbs to the dough for a savory variation that pairs well with soups and stews.

Gluten-Free Cornbread

Preparation Time: 10 minutes
Cooking Time: 20-25 minutes
Servings: 9 pieces

Ingredients

- 1 cup gluten-free sourdough discard
- 1 cup gluten-free cornmeal
- ½ cup gluten-free all-purpose flour (with xanthan gum)
- 1 tbsp sugar (optional, for a slightly sweet cornbread)
- 1 tsp baking powder
- ½ tsp baking soda
- ½ tsp salt
- 2 large eggs
- ½ cup almond milk (or milk of choice)
- ¼ cup melted butter or oil (for dairy-free option)

Directions

1. **Preheat Oven:**
   Preheat your oven to 400°F (200°C). Grease an 8x8-inch baking dish or line it with parchment paper.

2. **Combine Dry Ingredients:**
   In a large mixing bowl, combine the cornmeal, gluten-free flour, sugar (if using), baking powder, baking soda, and salt. Stir well to ensure even distribution of ingredients.

3. **Whisk Wet Ingredients:**
   In a separate bowl, whisk together the sourdough discard, eggs, milk, and melted butter. This step helps incorporate the flavors and ensures the cornbread will be moist.

4. **Mix Dry and Wet Ingredients:**
   Pour the wet mixture into the bowl with the dry ingredients, stirring until just combined. Avoid over-mixing, as this can make the cornbread dense.

5. **Pour into Baking Dish:**
   Pour the batter into the prepared baking dish, spreading it evenly to the edges.

6. **Bake:**
   Bake for 20-25 minutes or until the top is golden brown and a toothpick inserted in the center comes out clean. The edges should be slightly crispy.

7. **Cool and Serve:**
   Let the cornbread cool for a few minutes before slicing. Serve warm with butter, honey, or your favorite spread.

Nutritional Values (per piece)

- Calories: 160 kcal
- Carbohydrates: 20g
- Protein: 3g
- Fat: 7g
- Fiber: 2g
- Sugar: 1g
- Sodium: 300mg

Tips & Tricks

- **Sweeter Variation:** For a sweeter cornbread, add an extra tablespoon of sugar or drizzle honey over the batter before baking.

- **Add-Ins:** Consider adding chopped jalapenos, shredded cheese, or corn kernels for added texture and flavor.
- **Storage:** Store leftovers in an airtight container at room temperature for up to 2 days or freeze for longer storage. Reheat slices in the oven for the best texture.

Gluten-Free Wraps

Preparation Time: 15 minutes
Cooking Time: 10 minutes
Servings: 6 wraps

Ingredients

- 1 cup gluten-free sourdough discard
- ¾ cup gluten-free all-purpose flour (with xanthan gum)
- ¼ cup tapioca starch
- ½ tsp salt
- 1 tsp olive oil
- ½ cup warm water (as needed to achieve dough consistency)

Directions

1. **Combine Dry Ingredients:**
   In a medium mixing bowl, whisk together the gluten-free flour, tapioca starch, and salt. This blend will give the wraps the elasticity and softness needed for easy rolling.
2. **Add Wet Ingredients:**
   Add the gluten-free sourdough discard and olive oil to the dry mixture. Gradually add warm water, a little at a time, until a soft dough forms. The dough should be pliable and not sticky; adjust with a small amount of extra flour if needed.
3. **Knead the Dough:**
   Turn the dough onto a lightly floured surface and knead for about 2-3 minutes. This step helps develop a smooth texture for the wraps, making them easier to roll out and handle.
4. **Divide and Roll Out:**
   Divide the dough into 6 equal portions. Roll each piece into a ball, then flatten and roll out into a thin circle (about 8 inches in diameter). Keep the thickness consistent to ensure even cooking.
5. **Cook the Wraps:**
   Preheat a non-stick skillet over medium heat. Place one wrap in the skillet and cook for 1-2 minutes on each side, or until light brown spots appear. Repeat for each wrap, stacking them on a plate and covering with a clean cloth to keep them soft and warm.
6. **Serve or Store:**
   Serve warm with your choice of fillings. Alternatively, let cool completely before storing in an airtight container in the refrigerator.

Nutritional Values (per wrap)

- Calories: 120 kcal
- Carbohydrates: 22g
- Protein: 2g
- Fat: 3g
- Fiber: 1g
- Sugar: 0g
- Sodium: 150mg

Tips & Tricks

- **Flour Adjustments:** If the dough is too sticky, add a little more tapioca starch. If it's too dry, add a few more drops of water until it reaches the desired consistency.

- **Flavor Variations:** Mix in garlic powder, herbs, or spices for extra flavor.

- **Storage Tips:** Store cooked wraps in the refrigerator for up to 3 days. To freeze, place parchment paper between each wrap, wrap in plastic, and store in a freezer-safe container. Reheat on a skillet before using to restore softness.

Gluten-Free Focaccia

Preparation Time: 20 minutes (plus 1 hour rising time)
Cooking Time: 25-30 minutes
Servings: 8 pieces

Ingredients

- 1 cup gluten-free sourdough discard
- 1 ½ cups gluten-free all-purpose flour (with xanthan gum)
- ½ cup tapioca starch
- 1 tsp salt
- 1 tsp sugar
- 1 tbsp active dry yeast
- 1 cup warm water
- 2 tbsp olive oil (plus extra for drizzling)
- Toppings: Fresh rosemary, sea salt, and sliced cherry tomatoes

Directions

1. **Activate the Yeast:**
   In a small bowl, mix warm water and sugar, then sprinkle in the active dry yeast. Let sit for 5-10 minutes until frothy. This ensures the yeast is activated and ready for rising.

2. **Prepare the Dough:**
   In a large mixing bowl, combine the gluten-free flour, tapioca starch, and salt. Add the sourdough discard, olive oil, and the activated yeast mixture, stirring until a dough forms. If it's too sticky, add a little extra flour until it reaches a soft, workable consistency.

3. **Knead and Rise:**
   Turn the dough onto a floured surface and gently knead for about 2-3 minutes. Transfer to an oiled bowl, cover with a damp cloth, and let it rise in a warm spot for about 1 hour or until doubled in size.

4. **Shape the Focaccia:**
   Preheat your oven to 400°F (200°C). Grease an 8x8-inch or 9x9-inch baking pan with olive oil. Turn the risen dough out into the pan and use your fingers to spread it evenly. Press your fingertips into the dough to create dimples across the surface.

5. **Add Toppings:**
   Drizzle a bit of olive oil over the surface, and sprinkle with fresh rosemary, sea salt, and sliced cherry tomatoes. Feel free to add any other favorite toppings for added flavor.

6. **Bake:**
   Place the focaccia in the preheated oven and bake for 25-30 minutes, or until golden brown on top. The edges

should be crispy, while the inside remains soft.

7. **Cool and Serve:**
Let the focaccia cool slightly before slicing. Serve warm as a side dish, or use it for sandwiches.

Nutritional Values (per piece)

- Calories: 180 kcal
- Carbohydrates: 28g
- Protein: 3g
- Fat: 6g
- Fiber: 2g
- Sugar: 1g
- Sodium: 350mg

Tips & Tricks

- **Herb Variations:** Add thyme, oregano, or basil for a different flavor profile.
- **Storage Tips:** Store leftovers in an airtight container at room temperature for up to 2 days. Reheat in the oven to refresh the texture.
- **Freezing Instructions:** Wrap individual slices in plastic wrap, place in a freezer bag, and freeze for up to a month. Thaw and reheat before serving.

Gluten-Free Pancakes

Preparation Time: 10 minutes
Cooking Time: 15 minutes
Servings: 10 pancakes

Ingredients

- 1 cup gluten-free sourdough discard
- ¾ cup gluten-free all-purpose flour (with xanthan gum)
- 2 tbsp sugar
- 1 tsp baking powder
- ½ tsp baking soda
- ¼ tsp salt
- 1 large egg
- ½ cup almond milk (or milk of choice)
- 2 tbsp melted butter or coconut oil (plus more for cooking)

Directions

1. **Combine Dry Ingredients:**
In a medium bowl, whisk together the gluten-free flour, sugar, baking powder, baking soda, and salt. This mixture provides the structure and fluffiness that makes pancakes light.

2. **Mix Wet Ingredients:**
In a separate bowl, whisk together the sourdough discard, egg, almond milk, and melted butter or coconut oil until smooth and well combined.

3. **Combine Wet and Dry Mixtures:**
Pour the wet ingredients into the bowl with the dry ingredients, gently stirring until just combined. Avoid over-mixing, as this can result in dense pancakes. Let the batter rest for a few minutes to allow the gluten-free flour to hydrate fully.

4. **Cook the Pancakes:**
Heat a non-stick skillet or griddle over medium heat and lightly grease with a small amount of butter or oil. Pour ¼ cup of batter onto the skillet

for each pancake, spacing them apart to allow for spreading. Cook for 2-3 minutes or until bubbles form on the surface, then flip and cook for an additional 1-2 minutes on the other side until golden brown.

5. **Serve Warm:**
   Transfer pancakes to a plate and cover to keep warm while cooking the remaining batter. Serve hot with your favorite toppings like maple syrup, fresh berries, or a sprinkle of powdered sugar.

Nutritional Values (per pancake)

- Calories: 90 kcal
- Carbohydrates: 12g
- Protein: 2g
- Fat: 3g
- Fiber: 1g
- Sugar: 1g
- Sodium: 150mg

Tips & Tricks

- **Texture Adjustment:** If the batter is too thick, add a little more milk until it reaches a pourable consistency.
- **Flavor Additions:** Add vanilla extract, cinnamon, or a handful of chocolate chips for extra flavor.
- **Storage and Reheating:** Store leftover pancakes in the refrigerator for up to 2 days or freeze for longer storage. Reheat in a toaster or on the stovetop for best results.

Gluten-Free Breakfast Muffins

Preparation Time: 15 minutes
Cooking Time: 20-25 minutes
Servings: 12 muffins

Ingredients

- 1 cup gluten-free sourdough discard
- 1 cup gluten-free all-purpose flour (with xanthan gum)
- ½ cup almond flour
- ½ cup sugar (or coconut sugar for a refined-sugar-free option)
- 1 tsp baking powder
- ½ tsp baking soda
- ½ tsp salt
- 1 tsp cinnamon
- 2 large eggs
- ½ cup almond milk (or milk of choice)
- ¼ cup melted coconut oil (or butter)
- 1 tsp vanilla extract
- Optional add-ins: ½ cup blueberries, chopped nuts, or chocolate chips

Directions

1. **Preheat Oven:**
   Preheat your oven to 375°F (190°C) and line a 12-cup muffin tin with paper liners or lightly grease with oil.

2. **Combine Dry Ingredients:**
   In a large mixing bowl, whisk together the gluten-free flour, almond flour, sugar, baking powder, baking soda, salt, and cinnamon.

3. **Mix Wet Ingredients:**
   In a separate bowl, whisk together the sourdough discard, eggs, almond milk, melted coconut oil, and vanilla extract until smooth and well incorporated.

4. **Combine Wet and Dry Ingredients:**
   Pour the wet ingredients into the dry ingredients, gently folding until just combined. Be careful not to over-mix, as this can make the muffins dense. If using add-ins like blueberries, nuts, or chocolate chips, fold them in gently at this stage.

5. **Fill Muffin Tin:**
   Divide the batter evenly among the 12 muffin cups, filling each about ¾ full to allow for rising.

6. **Bake:**
   Place the muffin tin in the preheated oven and bake for 20-25 minutes or until a toothpick inserted into the center of a muffin comes out clean. The tops should be golden and firm to the touch.

7. **Cool and Serve:**
   Let the muffins cool in the tin for a few minutes before transferring to a wire rack to cool completely. Enjoy warm or at room temperature.

Nutritional Values (per muffin)
- Calories: 140 kcal
- Carbohydrates: 18g
- Protein: 3g
- Fat: 6g
- Fiber: 2g
- Sugar: 8g
- Sodium: 180mg

Tips & Tricks
- **Flavor Variations:** Try adding a teaspoon of lemon zest for a fresh twist, or swap the cinnamon for pumpkin spice for a seasonal flavor.
- **Storage Tips:** Store leftover muffins in an airtight container at room temperature for up to 2 days, or refrigerate for longer freshness. They can also be frozen for up to a month; just thaw and reheat as needed.
- **Healthier Options:** For a lower-sugar version, reduce the sugar by half or replace it with a natural sweetener like honey or maple syrup.

CONCLUSION

The journey through sourdough discard has shown just how versatile and resourceful baking can be when we embrace a zero-waste mindset. Every recipe in this book was crafted not just to satisfy cravings but to celebrate sustainable, nutritious, and family-friendly meals and treats. Using sourdough discard as a key ingredient allows us to turn what might have been waste into a valuable source of flavor and texture that brings an extra layer of depth to everything from morning pancakes to evening focaccia.

As a busy mom or family cook, it's easy to feel overwhelmed by the time, energy, and resources required to put wholesome food on the table. This cookbook aims to alleviate that burden, providing recipes that not only fit into a packed schedule but also offer the satisfaction of creating something special from scratch. With each chapter, you've been equipped with simple yet impactful tools and techniques that showcase sourdough discard's potential. From breakfast delights that bring warmth to mornings to savory snacks perfect for family gatherings, every recipe is a step toward a more sustainable kitchen.

Reflections on Zero-Waste Baking

Baking with sourdough discard isn't just about eliminating waste; it's a movement toward mindful cooking. This zero-waste approach is about more than ingredients—it's about rethinking how we can use, reuse, and repurpose. Each time you reach for your sourdough discard instead of discarding it, you contribute to a broader impact, cutting down on waste and maximizing the nutritional value of every meal.

This book was designed to give you tools to nurture that mindset. Whether it's baking a batch of gluten-free wraps for a quick lunch or whipping up a sweet treat like blueberry muffins for your family, you're showing that cooking from scratch with resourcefulness can be a joy rather than a chore.

Creating Moments Around the Table

Food has a unique power to bring people together, especially when it's homemade with intention and care. Each recipe here is an opportunity to create moments with those you love. Whether it's the simple satisfaction of your kids enjoying freshly baked gluten-free bagels on a weekend morning or the shared pride in creating that perfect batch of sourdough pretzels, these recipes bring families closer around the table.

Encourage kids, friends, and partners to join you in the kitchen whenever possible. Cooking together makes the journey memorable and helps to pass on a love for sustainable, home-cooked food to the next generation. As they grow, they'll carry forward the knowledge and joy of zero-waste cooking, knowing the value of each ingredient and the care that goes into every meal.

Beyond the Recipes

The lessons in this book go beyond just cooking. They extend to the principles of sustainable living, resourcefulness, and creativity. With the methods you've practiced here, you can approach other ingredients in your kitchen with a similar zero-waste mentality. Leftover vegetables can become soups, scraps can make broths, and "unusable" parts of food can often be transformed with a bit of creativity.

In addition, feel free to experiment with these recipes, customizing them to your family's preferences or dietary needs. Recipes, after all, are just starting points, and sourdough discard is versatile enough to be incorporated into countless dishes beyond what's in this book. Try different flours, add spices, swap in seasonal ingredients, or even adapt the methods for your own signature dishes. Every experiment adds to your kitchen skills and makes cooking more rewarding.

Final Thoughts on Sourdough Discard

As you continue to bake with sourdough discard, remember the journey it represents. It's a humble ingredient, often overlooked, yet it holds the potential to elevate both simple meals and decadent treats. Sourdough discard connects us to the age-old tradition of fermentation, to the balance of flavors that have sustained families for generations, and to a sustainable future where food is valued fully.

Thank you for choosing to make a difference in your kitchen. As you bake, create, and innovate, you're helping to shape a more mindful and resourceful way of living. May this cookbook serve as a lasting guide on your zero-waste baking journey, inspiring delicious memories, sustainable practices, and an appreciation for every ingredient. Here's to the joy of baking, the love of family meals, and the incredible possibilities that sourdough discard brings to your table.

SCAN THE QR CODE BELOW TO GET ACCESS TO YOUR BONUSES

SCAN ME

Printed in Great Britain
by Amazon